MELANIA TRUMP NEV

THE EXTRAORDINARY LIFE AND REAL STORY OF MELANIA THAT YOU NEVER KNEW

LARA MULL

Copyright © LARA MULL, 2024

All rights reserved. No part of this publication may be reproduced, distributed, or transmitted in any form or by any means, including photocopying, recording, or other electronic or mechanical methods, without the prior written permission of the publisher, except in the case of brief quotations embodied in critical reviews and certain other noncommercial uses permitted by copyright law.

CONTENTS

Introduction

Melania Trump Makes a Daring Return Amid Political Tensions 6
Beyond the Headlines 7
  ○ The public's perception vs. the private reality 8
  ○ Why this memoir is different 9
Chapter 1 10
  From Novo Mesto to New York
  The Journey of a Small-Town Girl to the World Stage 10
  Childhood in Slovenia: Shaped by a different world 10
  Navigating early ambitions: Modeling as an escape 11
  First steps toward a new life in America 12
Chapter 2 14
  The Rise of a Fashion Icon 14
  Modeling Dreams, American Realities 14
  ○ Life as a young model: The highs and lows 14
  ○ Breaking into New York's cutthroat fashion industry 16
Chapter 3 20
Crossing Paths with Power 20
Melania and Donald Trump—A High-Stakes Union 20
  ○ A fateful meeting in the city that never sleeps 20
      Romance, Public Scrutiny, and a Bond with the Future President 22
  ○ The untold dynamics of their relationship 24
Chapter 4 28
  Navigating Life in the Public Eye
  The Making of a Private First Lady 28
  ○ Marriage, motherhood, and managing Trump's empire 28
  ○ Balancing personal identity with the Trump brand 31
  ○ The sacrifices and rewards of life in the spotlight 33
Chapter 5 37
Behind the White House Walls
Melania's Silent Strength and Unseen Struggles 37
  ○ How she dealt with critics, rumors, and the media frenzy 41
Chapter 6 44
Be Best—The First Lady's Mission 44
Championing Causes Amid Media Storms 44

- ○ "Be Best": Melania's signature initiative for children..........44
- ○ What the program represented—and how it was perceived..........46
- ○ Juggling public service with private doubts..........48

Chapter 7..........51
The Public vs. The Private Melania..........51
Who Is She Really? The Dichotomy of Perception..........51
- ○ Public Melania: The poised and polished image..........51
- ○ Private Melania: Stories from those who know her behind the scenes..........53
- ○ A woman shaped by complex contradictions..........55

Chapter 8..........58
The Exit—Life After the White House..........58
Retreating from the Spotlight and Redefining Herself..........58
- ○ A quiet departure: Melania's reflections on leaving power..........60
- ○ Life beyond the White House: What comes next?..........60
- ○ Reclaiming her narrative in a post-political world..........62

Influence, Impact, and the Road Ahead..........64
- ○ The Melania Trump legacy: More than just a footnote..........67

Conclusion..........71
A Portrait of Resilience..........71
The Unwritten Chapters of Melania Trump's Story..........71

Introduction

Melania Trump Makes a Daring Return Amid Political Tensions

In a rare public appearance, Melania Trump stepped into the spotlight at the Republican National Convention in Milwaukee, making her first notable entrance since the attempted assassination of her husband, Donald Trump. Sporting a vibrant Republican red dress, she entered the venue to the elegant strains of classical music, a refreshing contrast to the lively country and rock tunes that had filled the space all week.

With her glamorous presence, Melania resembled a model on a runway more than a political figure navigating the complexities of a national convention. Her demeanor remained characteristically composed and somewhat distant as she joined her husband on stage following his lengthy acceptance speech. The moment was marked by an embrace and a brief kiss on the cheek before they walked hand in hand across the stage, flanked by their family.

Throughout Donald Trump's presidency, Melania has redefined the role of First Lady, often choosing a path of solitude and discretion. In the White House, she was less visible compared to previous First Ladies, prioritizing specific interests, particularly her advocacy for children. The U.S. National Archives once referred to her as an "ambassador for kindness," underscoring her focus on nurturing initiatives.

Since leaving office, her public appearances have dwindled. Notably, she opted out of significant moments in Donald Trump's life, including his recent mugshot and conviction in New York, raising eyebrows and speculation about her intentions. Observers have noted that Melania is a woman who charts her own course, refusing to adhere to expectations.

"She does what she wants," remarked Mary Jordan, author of *The Art of Her Deal*. "Melania is fiercely independent and not bound by traditional obligations."

Her absence during pivotal moments was felt at the convention when Donald Trump received an enthusiastic welcome from supporters, heralded for surviving a recent assassination attempt. When Melania finally appeared, her timing was eagerly awaited by convention-goers who had been anticipating her presence.

In a rare statement following the shooting incident, Melania offered a glimpse into her thoughts, describing the assailant as a "monster" who failed to see the human side of her husband. She emphasized his character beyond the political persona, portraying him as a loving and generous man who has shared both the highs and lows of life with her.

Unlike the customary tradition of spouses delivering heartfelt anecdotes at political conventions, Melania has chosen to remain silent, opting out of speaking engagements altogether. While other members of the Trump family took to the stage to share their stories, she refrained, exemplifying her determination to maintain her autonomy.

Her previous attempt to introduce her husband at the 2016 convention was marred by controversy, with accusations of plagiarism against Michelle Obama's speech. This experience may have further solidified her decision to avoid the spotlight during significant events.

Melania understands the art of image and presence, drawing on her background as a former model. By limiting her appearances, she heightens the impact of each one. Her reclusive nature has cultivated an air of mystique that keeps the public intrigued.

After her husband's assassination attempt, her absence was notable, but her subsequent entrance at the convention signaled her ability to command attention when she chooses. As she ascended to the VIP section, pausing to acknowledge the crowd, Melania illustrated her skill in wielding the power of visual representation.

In navigating her role, she continues to walk a fine line, balancing the complexities of public expectation with her desire for privacy. Melania Trump's presence—or absence—reminds us that, in the world of politics, both can hold significant weight.

Beyond the Headlines

Unveiling the Woman Behind the Glamour

It was a crisp autumn evening in Washington, D.C., a night when history was about to be made. As the world anxiously awaited the results of the 2016 election, all eyes were glued to the television, tracking every update. In the Trump Tower penthouse, surrounded by luxury, Melania Trump stood by a window, gazing at the city lights below. The world had cast her as a supporting role in the political drama unfolding, but in this quiet moment, Melania was wrestling with a truth few could understand.

She had never sought the spotlight, yet here she was, standing on the verge of becoming the First Lady of the United States.

A small smile touched her lips as she heard the door open behind her. It was Donald, his usual confident stride breaking the silence. "It's happening," he said, a rare touch of emotion in his voice. She nodded but said nothing, feeling the weight of a role she never imagined playing. The opulent surroundings suddenly felt stifling. The world would soon see her on that victory stage, but they wouldn't see the woman behind the carefully curated image—the woman who had lived a life far removed from the lights and cameras now about to consume her.

Former First Lady Melania Trump recently made a rare public appearance at the National Archives in Washington, D.C., where she spoke about her personal experience with the U.S. immigration process. During the naturalization ceremony, she addressed 25 new citizens and shared insights into the challenges immigrants face while pursuing citizenship.

Melania, who became a U.S. citizen in 2006, recounted her journey through the immigration system. "My experience opened my eyes to the realities faced by those seeking to become U.S. citizens," she said. She emphasized the difficulties of navigating immigration law, explaining that her journey involved extensive research and organizing complex paperwork. "The pathway to citizenship can feel like a labyrinth," she noted, reflecting on the struggles many encounter.

This appearance comes during a politically charged time, as her husband, Donald Trump, is actively campaigning for the presidency while facing legal issues. Melania did not mention him during her speech, but sources close to her indicated that she has his full support for participating in the ceremony.

Meeting with U.S. Archivist Colleen Shogan, who extended the invitation to Melania, she expressed that it was an honor to be there. Since leaving the White House in January 2021, Melania has chosen to maintain a relatively private life, focusing on her family and especially their son, Barron, who is approaching high school graduation.

While she has not been a frequent presence on the campaign trail, she has voiced her support for Donald Trump's political efforts. In recent interviews, she stated, "I am looking forward to a hopeful future for our country."

Although her husband hinted that Melania might join him on the campaign trail in the future, he acknowledged her preference for a more private life, saying, "She loves our country and prefers to stay away from the negativity."

Melania Trump's remarks during the naturalization ceremony provide valuable insights into her own journey and highlight the immigrant experience in America.

- ### The public's perception vs. the private reality.

From the moment she stepped onto the global stage, Melania Trump became a canvas for public imagination. To some, she was the mysterious beauty, perfectly poised beside one of the world's most controversial figures. To others, she was an enigma—her quiet demeanor sparking endless speculation about who she really was beneath the glamorous exterior.

The media focused on her stoic expressions, her elegant style, and the occasional glimpse of a seemingly strained smile. Headlines painted her as a reluctant First Lady, cast unwillingly into a role she neither asked for nor embraced. Critics labeled her as distant, detached, and out of touch, while admirers celebrated her grace and calm under pressure.

But behind the layers of designer gowns and staged photo ops lies a woman far more complex than the headlines suggest. Melania has navigated a life filled with contradictions: a private soul in an overwhelmingly public world, an immigrant who became the First Lady of a fiercely nationalist administration, and a devoted mother fiercely protective of her son, Barron, while remaining a figure of global intrigue.

While the world speculated about her feelings toward her husband's policies, the marriage itself, or her views on politics, Melania's true reality was something few were privy to. In private, she was reflective, often meditative, holding conversations with only a trusted circle. Her quietness wasn't detachment, but a deliberate choice to keep parts of herself shielded from a public hungry for every detail.

She wasn't just an ornament in the Trump administration, nor was she simply following in the footsteps of previous First Ladies. In truth, Melania was crafting her own path, but doing so in the shadows, where most never dared to look.

- ### Why this memoir is different.

In the sea of articles, interviews, and speculation surrounding Melania Trump, one truth remains clear: few people really know her. From glossy magazine covers to harsh opinion pieces, Melania has been both idealized and criticized. But most narratives have focused on the surface—her fashion, her silence, her role as the wife of a controversial president. This memoir, however, dives deeper.

Rather than repeating the same public narratives, this book pulls back the curtain on the complexities of Melania's life. It's not just about what the cameras captured, but what they missed. It's a journey through her personal evolution, her quiet resilience, and the life she built long before and after the White House.

What makes this memoir different is that it offers three key dimensions:

- **A biographical deep dive** into her roots, tracing her journey from Slovenia to becoming one of the most recognizable women in the world.
- **An investigative lens**, exploring the unseen power dynamics of her role as First Lady, challenging assumptions, and uncovering untold stories from behind the scenes.
- **A personal reflection**, blending rare insights into her private thoughts, struggles, and victories as she balanced public duty with personal identity.

This is not just another story about a First Lady. This is a journey into the heart of a woman who has lived through the highest peaks and darkest valleys of fame and power—yet still remains, in many ways, an enigma. It's time to meet the real Melania.

Chapter 1

From Novo Mesto to New York
The Journey of a Small-Town Girl to the World Stage

Childhood in Slovenia: Shaped by a different world.

Before the skyscrapers of New York and the opulence of the White House, there was a small industrial town nestled in the rolling hills of Slovenia. Novo Mesto, where Melania Knauss was born, was a far cry from the world of luxury and power she would one day inhabit. The Cold War-era landscape was one of modesty and restraint, where the dreams of young girls were often tempered by the harsh realities of life behind the Iron Curtain.

Growing up in Yugoslavia, Melania's early life was shaped by a world of contrasts. Her father, a car dealer with a strong work ethic, provided a stable foundation, while her mother, who worked in a local textile factory, ignited Melania's love for fashion and aesthetics. In their home, there was an emphasis on discipline, ambition, and the importance of making one's way in life through hard work.

But it wasn't all struggle. There was beauty in the simplicity of Slovenian life—long summers spent in the countryside, family gatherings that celebrated tradition, and an unspoken resilience that came from living in a place often overshadowed by global powers. As a young girl, Melania learned to observe more than she spoke. In a world where political tensions ran high, silence was often a means of survival.

Yet, even from an early age, there was a sense that Melania was destined for more. Tall, graceful, and with an innate sense of style, she quickly outgrew the provincial life of her childhood. She would look at glossy magazines, her imagination taking her far beyond the borders of her small town. In those moments, she was already crafting a different reality for herself, one that would one day take her far from the familiar streets of Novo Mesto.

The world she was born into may have been one of limitations, but Melania was always quietly determined to transcend those boundaries. And transcend what she did, though the lessons of that early life in Slovenia—the resilience, the discipline, the understated ambition—would remain with her long after she left.

Navigating early ambitions: Modeling as an escape.

As Melania Knauss entered her teenage years, the modest streets of Sevnica felt smaller with each passing day. The weight of her ambitions began to outgrow the boundaries of her small Slovenian town, where options were limited, and dreams beyond the everyday grind were often dismissed as unattainable. But for Melania, escape was not just a dream—it was a necessity.

From an early age, Melania's striking beauty and statuesque figure caught the attention of those around her. Her angular features, coupled with an innate grace, made her stand out in a way that went beyond mere aesthetics. Yet it wasn't vanity that drove her; it was a quiet determination, a belief that she could carve out a different future for herself.

At 16, she entered the world of modeling—an industry that offered a rare ticket out of Slovenia. She began with local fashion shows and photo shoots, where her natural poise in front of the camera set her apart. But it was in those moments under the flashbulbs and spotlights that she discovered something deeper: a sense of freedom. The camera lens became a portal to another world—one where the limitations of her upbringing faded, and she could project the image of the woman she wanted to become.

Modeling, for Melania, wasn't just a profession; it was an escape from the constraints of her environment. Each pose, each step on the runway was a step closer to a life she envisioned for herself—one where she would control her own destiny. She honed her craft with precision, understanding that this was her key to a life far beyond Sevnica.

Despite the glamor and opportunity that modeling offered, it was not without its challenges. The competitive world of fashion demanded resilience. Rejection was a common part of the process, and Melania, with her quiet demeanor, had to develop a thick skin. Still, her discipline—ingrained since childhood—served her well. She knew how to bide her time, to endure the setbacks in silence while keeping her eye on the larger goal.

By the time she turned 18, Melania's modeling career had grown beyond Slovenia's borders. She began to work internationally, traveling to cities like Milan and Paris—places that once seemed as distant as a dream. But it wasn't just about the clothes or the fame; modeling became her means of constructing a new reality. With every photo shoot, every fashion show, she was building the life she had long imagined, one where she was no longer confined to her origins but defined by her aspirations.

The fashion industry gave Melania something she had long yearned for: control over her narrative. She could curate the image she projected to the world, choosing when to speak and, more often, when to remain silent. This mastery of presentation would serve her well in the years to come, when the world would demand to know more about the woman beside Donald Trump.

But for now, modeling offered Melania something even more precious than control: the promise of escape, and the chance to redefine herself on her own terms.

First steps toward a new life in America.

In the summer of 1996, Melania Knauss stood at a crossroads, one that would forever alter the trajectory of her life. Having made a name for herself as a successful model in Europe, she faced a pivotal decision: to stay in the familiar embrace of her homeland or to leap into the unknown of America—a land brimming with possibilities but fraught with uncertainties.

The allure of the United States was undeniable. For Melania, it represented more than just a new country; it symbolized freedom and the chance to fulfill her long-held dreams. She envisioned a place where her aspirations could flourish without the constraints of her upbringing. With the support of a modeling agency that saw potential in her unique beauty and grace, Melania packed her bags and boarded a plane to New York City, ready to embark on a journey that would shape her future.

Upon arrival, the vibrant chaos of New York was a stark contrast to the tranquil life she had known in Slovenia. The city pulsed with energy, a dizzying blend of cultures, languages, and aspirations. For a girl who had spent her formative years in a small town, the towering skyscrapers and fast-paced lifestyle felt both exhilarating and overwhelming. Yet, amid the noise and rush, Melania felt an undeniable spark of excitement. This was her moment, a chance to immerse herself in a world she had only seen in magazines and on television.

Initially, the challenges were daunting. Melania faced a new language and an unfamiliar culture, where the pace of life left little room for hesitation. She quickly learned that in the fashion capital of the world, success was fiercely competitive. The industry was not just about beauty; it demanded grit, determination, and a willingness to adapt. Melania, with her strong work ethic and relentless ambition, embraced these challenges head-on.

As she navigated her way through the bustling streets, she found herself attending castings and networking events, all while immersing herself in the vibrant social scene of New York. It was here that she discovered the power of connections and the importance of building a brand around herself. She learned to market her unique background, using her Eastern European roots to stand out in a city overflowing with models. Each opportunity she seized brought her one step closer to her ultimate goal.

During this time, she also began to understand the nuances of American culture—its complexity, its contradictions. In her interactions with photographers, designers, and fellow models, she witnessed the American dream in action, a testament to the belief that anyone, regardless of their background, could achieve success with hard work and determination. Melania embraced this ethos, determined to carve out her own path in this vast, new landscape.

Yet, amidst the glitz and glamor of New York, there were moments of solitude. She often reflected on her family back in Slovenia, the distance amplifying her sense of longing. The support of her parents had been instrumental in her journey, instilling in her the confidence to pursue her dreams. Even as she thrived in her new life, the values they had imparted—discipline, resilience, and humility—remained her guiding principles.

With each passing day, Melania began to forge her identity in America, blending her Slovenian roots with the aspirations of a burgeoning modeling career. The first steps into this new life were not without hurdles, but they were also filled with promise. As she embraced the challenges and opportunities, the girl from Novo Mesto was evolving into a woman poised to redefine her narrative.

Chapter 2

The Rise of a Fashion Icon

Modeling Dreams, American Realities

- #### Life as a young model: The highs and lows.

As Melania Knauss stepped further into the modeling world, she quickly discovered a landscape painted with both dazzling highs and disheartening lows. The industry was a whirlwind—a world where success was measured in castings, bookings, and the ephemeral nature of beauty.

The Highs: Glamor and Opportunity

In those early years, the high points of Melania's modeling career were intoxicating. She found herself walking runways in Paris and Milan, gracing the pages of high-fashion magazines, and collaborating with renowned photographers and designers. Each assignment was a chance to showcase her unique blend of European elegance and fierce ambition, and she quickly garnered attention for her poise and striking features.

One of her first major breaks came when she was cast for a campaign with a prominent Italian fashion brand. The excitement of being photographed by a celebrated photographer and wearing designs that were the pinnacle of fashion filled her with a sense of accomplishment. Each click of the camera validated her choice to leave her home and pursue her dreams in America.

Social events and parties accompanied these successes, offering glimpses into a glamorous lifestyle that felt almost surreal. Melania mingled with celebrities, attended lavish galas, and celebrated milestones with fellow models and designers. She reveled in the thrill of it all, the sparkling lights, and the intoxicating energy of New York's fashion scene. These experiences solidified her belief that she was meant for this world—a belief that fueled her ambitions and kept her pushing forward.

The Lows: Rejection and Insecurity

Yet, beneath the glitzy facade lay a harsher reality. The modeling industry, while glamorous, was also ruthlessly competitive. Rejection became a frequent companion, and Melania quickly learned that even the most promising opportunities could evaporate in an instant. She faced countless castings where she was told she was "not the right fit" or "too tall" or "too thin." Each "no" chipped away at her confidence, forcing her to confront the fickle nature of beauty and public perception.

In moments of solitude, Melania wrestled with self-doubt. The constant comparison to other models, many of whom were equally striking, left her questioning her worth. While she projected confidence on the runway, the pressure to maintain that image often felt overwhelming. She found solace in her work ethic, reminding herself that persistence was key.

Moreover, the lifestyle of a young model brought its own set of challenges. Long hours, demanding schedules, and the pressure to maintain a certain physique often led to exhaustion. The pursuit of perfection became an unrelenting cycle, where self-care was sometimes sacrificed for the sake of appearances. Melania adopted strict dietary regimens and workout routines to meet the industry's expectations, pushing herself to the limits to ensure she remained in demand.

Finding Balance: Strength in Vulnerability

Despite the ups and downs, Melania began to understand the importance of resilience. Each setback became a learning opportunity, a chance to reassess her goals and strengthen her resolve. She sought support from fellow models who faced similar struggles, forging friendships that offered camaraderie amid the chaos. These connections became invaluable as they navigated the complexities of their shared experiences in an industry that could often feel isolating.

Through these challenges, Melania also learned the art of reinvention. Each photoshoot allowed her to explore different facets of her personality, expressing herself in ways that transcended mere appearances. She began to embrace her unique background, incorporating her Slovenian heritage into her work, which set her apart in an industry that often favored the conventional.

With time, Melania transformed her early insecurities into a source of strength. She emerged not just as a model, but as a multifaceted individual—a woman who could balance ambition with authenticity.

Life as a young model was a tumultuous journey, filled with both the exhilarating highs of fashion's glamor and the sobering lows of rejection. Yet, through it all, Melania forged a path that would not only define her career but lay the foundation for the woman she was destined to become.

- Breaking into New York's cutthroat fashion industry.

For Melania Knauss, arriving in New York City marked the beginning of an exhilarating and arduous journey through the cutthroat world of fashion. With a mere suitcase filled with clothes and a heart full of ambition, she stepped into an industry notorious for its fierce competition, demanding standards, and unforgiving nature.

The Urban Jungle: A New Frontier

As she navigated the sprawling streets of Manhattan, Melania was acutely aware that she was one of many aspiring models vying for the attention of casting directors, photographers, and designers. The city, a pulsating hub of creativity and commerce, was also a ruthless arena where talent was scrutinized, and the spotlight shifted with dizzying speed.

To break through this urban jungle, Melania understood that she needed more than just good looks; she had to develop a strategy. She began by immersing herself in the culture of the fashion industry, studying the trends, the players, and the intricacies of the business. She attended every casting call she could find, honing her ability to adapt to different styles and presentations. Each rejection, rather than discouraging her, became a lesson in resilience and determination.

Building Connections: The Power of Networking

Networking proved crucial in her journey. Melania learned quickly that the fashion world was as much about relationships as it was about talent. She began to cultivate connections with photographers, stylists, and fellow models, attending events and parties that could open doors. These social gatherings provided an invaluable opportunity to meet industry insiders and gain insights into the often-secretive workings of fashion.

One of her key breakthroughs came when she caught the eye of a prominent photographer at a modeling event. He recognized her potential and offered her a chance to collaborate on a project that would showcase her unique style and presence. This opportunity marked a turning point in her career, providing her with exposure to influential figures within the industry and establishing her as a name worth watching.

The Reality of Competition: Rising Above the Noise

However, the road was fraught with challenges. As Melania attended casting calls, she faced the stark reality of competition. The waiting rooms were filled with other beautiful models, each striving for the same coveted spots. The pressure to stand out was palpable, with whispers of favorites and insiders dominating the atmosphere. In this environment, it was essential for Melania to maintain her composure and confidence, even when surrounded by fierce competition.

To distinguish herself, she leaned into her heritage, embracing her Slovenian roots. Melania presented herself not just as another model, but as an embodiment of a different kind of beauty—one that was both exotic and relatable. Her unique background became her asset, allowing her to appeal to a wider array of clients looking for something fresh and distinctive.

The Art of Adaptation: Navigating the Industry's Demands

Success in New York's fashion industry required adaptation. Melania learned the importance of versatility, mastering different looks and styles to meet the demands of diverse clients. She embraced the fast-paced lifestyle, often juggling multiple bookings in a single day, leaving little room for fatigue. The early mornings and late nights became the norm as she honed her craft, preparing herself for the demands of an industry that rarely paused for breath.

Moreover, Melania had to navigate the shifting dynamics of beauty standards and fashion trends, which often felt like an ever-moving target. The pressure to stay relevant was constant. With each season, new faces emerged, and older models risked being sidelined. To counter this, Melania invested time in her physical and mental well-being. She cultivated a disciplined routine that included workouts and healthy eating, ensuring that she was always at her best when it mattered most.

Finding Her Voice: A Model with Purpose

As she broke deeper into the fashion scene, Melania began to find her voice—not just as a model, but as a woman with opinions and values. She sought out opportunities that aligned with her personal beliefs, using her platform to advocate for causes she cared about, such as children's health and education. This newfound sense of purpose added depth to her identity, setting her apart in an industry often criticized for its superficiality.

Breaking into New York's cutthroat fashion industry was not just a career move for Melania; it was a transformative experience. Each casting call, collaboration, and connection fortified her resolve and sharpened her skills. As she faced the highs and lows, the glamor and the grind, Melania was evolving—not just into a successful model, but into a determined woman ready to take on whatever challenges lay ahead.

- **What the camera captured—and what it missed.**

In the world of modeling, the camera serves as both a window and a barrier, capturing fleeting moments while obscuring the complexities behind them. For Melania Knauss, this duality was profoundly evident as she navigated her burgeoning career in the fashion industry during the late 1990s and early 2000s.

Moments in the Spotlight: 1996-2001

On April 20, 1996, Melania made her New York runway debut for the fashion label *Karin*. Dressed in a striking black gown that accentuated her figure, she captivated the audience and set the stage for her ascent in the industry. Her poise and confidence on that stage were palpable; as she later recalled in an interview, "When I walked out there, I felt like I was flying. The energy was incredible."

As she secured more runway shows, Melania became a sought-after name in the fashion scene. In September 1997, she walked for *Marc Bouwer* during New York Fashion Week, a pivotal event that caught the attention of major fashion magazines. Photographed by *Patrick Demarchelier*, the images encapsulated not just her beauty but the ethereal quality that defined her runway presence. This event was significant—not just for her career but also for solidifying her status as a rising star.

Melania's first major magazine feature came in the *September 1999 issue of *Vanity Fair*, where she was photographed by the iconic *Annie Leibovitz*. The editorial showcased her elegance and allure, presenting her as a woman who could command attention in any setting. However, the accompanying article glossed over her personal journey, focusing instead on her relationships within the industry.

Behind the Lens: The Stories Untold

While the camera captured Melania's polished exterior, it often missed the deeper narratives that shaped her. The long hours spent preparing for photoshoots, the constant pressure to maintain a certain image, and the pervasive sense of competition were seldom seen in the glamorous images that filled magazine spreads.

For instance, during a high-profile shoot for *Vogue* in 2001, Melania experienced a moment of vulnerability that contrasted starkly with her poised public persona. After a grueling day under the bright lights and constant adjustments, she found herself questioning whether she truly belonged in such an elite circle. As she later reflected, "The camera can capture beauty, but it can't capture the doubt that sometimes sits within you."

This inner turmoil was compounded by the intense scrutiny from the media. Melania faced relentless comparisons to other models and celebrities, each remark weighing heavily on her self-esteem. Despite her success, the constant spotlight often felt more like a magnifying glass, revealing not just her triumphs but also her insecurities.

A Turning Point: The 2004 Fashion Week Experience

A pivotal moment came during *New York Fashion Week* in September 2004 when Melania was invited to walk for *Vera Wang*. This opportunity placed her in the same lineup as iconic models such as *Naomi Campbell* and *Tyra Banks*. As she walked the runway, the world watched, but few understood the years of hard work and resilience that had led her to that moment.

That night, her signature look—a sleek updo paired with a breathtaking gown—took the fashion world by storm. Photographers captured her in a way that reflected her newfound confidence and mastery of the runway. Yet, behind the scenes, she felt a mixture of excitement and anxiety, realizing that such moments were fleeting. "You have to be ready for the next big thing," she said in a post-show interview. "One moment you're on top, and the next, you're yesterday's news."

The Other Side of Fame: Building a Personal Life

Amidst the flashing cameras and the relentless pace of fashion, Melania yearned for a semblance of normalcy. In 2005, she met Donald Trump at a *New York Fashion Week* party, and their ensuing relationship became a focal point of media attention. Photographers captured their glamorous outings, but what remained unseen was Melania's struggle to navigate the complexities of dating one of the world's most famous figures.

In interviews, she would later say, "People saw the glitz, but they didn't see the sacrifices I had to make for our relationship." As their romance blossomed, Melania grappled with balancing her burgeoning modeling career and the public interest in her personal life.

The Balance of Image and Reality

Through her journey in the fashion industry, Melania learned to navigate the duality of being both a public figure and a private individual. The camera may have captured her beauty and the glamor of the runway, but it often overlooked the sacrifices, doubts, and the hard work that lay beneath the surface.

As she continued to evolve as a model and a woman, Melania embraced her complexities, understanding that her story was not just one of glitz and glamor, but one of resilience, ambition, and the pursuit of authenticity in a world that often demanded perfection.

Chapter 3

Crossing Paths with Power

Melania and Donald Trump—A High-Stakes Union

○ A fateful meeting in the city that never sleeps.

The neon lights of New York City blazed like stars in a man-made galaxy, illuminating the night with a vibrancy that pulsed through the streets. It was September 2005, and as fashion week buzzed with energy, Melania Knauss found herself immersed in the whirlwind of parties, shows, and exclusive events. Little did she know, one fateful evening would change the course of her life forever.

The Setting: A Night of Glamour

On a balmy night, Melania attended a lavish party hosted by *Vanity Fair* to celebrate the latest issue featuring top designers and models. The air was thick with excitement as influential figures mingled, sipping champagne and discussing the latest trends. Melania, dressed in a stunning *black cocktail dress* that accentuated her figure, effortlessly caught the attention of onlookers. Her presence was magnetic, a blend of elegance and intrigue that made her a standout amidst the crowd.

As she navigated the glamorous gathering, she noticed a familiar figure across the room—Donald Trump. The real estate mogul was surrounded by admirers, his larger-than-life personality drawing people in. Melania had seen him in the tabloids and on television, but she had never met him in person. With curiosity piqued, she felt an inexplicable pull toward him.

The Encounter: Sparks Fly

Taking a deep breath, Melania approached Trump. As their eyes met, time seemed to stand still. They exchanged pleasantries, and what began as a casual conversation quickly turned into an engaging dialogue. Donald, ever the charmer, expressed genuine interest in her background and her career. He marveled at her journey from Slovenia to becoming a rising star in the modeling world.

"Tell me about your experience in New York," he said, leaning in with an earnestness that surprised her. "It must be quite the adventure."

Melania found herself opening up about her struggles in the industry—the rejections, the late nights, the relentless pursuit of success. "It's a beautiful chaos," she replied with a smile, her eyes sparkling with passion. "But every challenge brings growth."

As the night wore on, their chemistry deepened. They shared laughter, exchanged dreams, and for the first time in a long while, Melania felt a connection that transcended the superficiality of the fashion world. Donald's charm and charisma captivated her, while she impressed him with her intelligence and ambition.

A Moment to Remember: The First Kiss

The party continued around them, but at that moment, it felt as though they were the only two people in the room. As the clock approached midnight, they found themselves stepping out onto the balcony, overlooking the glittering skyline. The city that never sleeps lay before them, a breathtaking tapestry of lights and possibilities.

With the cool night breeze swirling around them, Donald took a step closer, his gaze intense. "You know," he said softly, "you're one of the most fascinating women I've ever met."

Melania's heart raced as she looked into his eyes, filled with a mix of uncertainty and excitement. The world seemed to fade away as he leaned in, capturing her lips in a soft, lingering kiss. It was a moment suspended in time, a pivotal encounter that would intertwine their lives in ways neither could have anticipated.

The Aftermath: A New Chapter Begins

In the days that followed, the whirlwind romance blossomed. They attended exclusive events together, and Melania was often seen by Donald's side at high-profile gatherings, each outing solidifying their connection. She was introduced to his world of power and influence—a stark contrast to the fashion circles she had known.

Despite the glamor and attention, Melania remained grounded. She was cautious, aware of the media's watchful eye. In a 2006 interview with *People Magazine*, she reflected on their relationship, stating, "Donald is not just a businessman; he's a visionary. He inspires me to think bigger and pursue my dreams without fear."

Yet, the intense scrutiny that came with being Donald Trump's girlfriend was a new challenge for Melania. The tabloids were relentless, speculating about their relationship and painting her in various lights—some flattering, others less so.

As their romance deepened, Melania began to recognize the complexities of her newfound life. The man she had fallen for was not just a figure in the spotlight; he was a powerful businessman with a world of responsibility on his shoulders. The stakes were higher, but so were the potential rewards.

A Love Story in the Making

Their fateful meeting in New York City marked the beginning of a love story that would captivate the world. As they navigated the challenges of their relationship, Melania found herself balancing her ambitions with the demands of a high-profile romance. She was no longer just a model; she was becoming part of a legacy, a narrative that would unfold over the years to come.

The camera captured the moments of their blossoming relationship—the glamorous events, the shared smiles, the fleeting glances—but what it often missed were the intimate conversations, the quiet moments of reflection, and the unwavering support they provided each other as they embarked on an extraordinary journey together.

Romance, Public Scrutiny, and a Bond with the Future President

As Melania and Donald Trump's romance blossomed, it quickly became a narrative woven into the fabric of American media. By early 2005, they were no longer just a couple; they were a sensation. Their love story, marked by glamorous public appearances and intimate moments, became a focal point for both admirers and critics alike.

A Love Story Unfolds

After their initial meeting at *Vanity Fair's* fashion week party in September 2005, Melania and Donald's relationship developed rapidly. The couple was spotted at various events, each sighting generating headlines and speculation. One significant moment came on January 7, 2006, when they attended the *Golden Globe Awards*. Photographers captured Melania in a breathtaking red gown designed by *Zac Posen*, exuding confidence as she walked hand in hand with Donald. Their chemistry was undeniable, and the media couldn't get enough of them.

In interviews, Donald expressed his admiration for Melania. "She's a remarkable woman," he would often say. "She understands the demands of my life and supports me unconditionally." For Melania, Donald represented not just a romantic partner, but also a mentor and a confidant. His ambition inspired her, and she admired his tenacity and vision.

The Weight of Public Scrutiny

However, the couple's fairy tale was overshadowed by intense public scrutiny. With each appearance, they faced relentless media attention, often dissecting their relationship and scrutinizing every detail of their lives. Tabloids speculated about the dynamics of their relationship, from the age difference—Melania was 24 years younger than Donald—to allegations about their pasts.

In interviews, Melania maintained a composed demeanor, acknowledging the challenges that came with the spotlight. "People see what they want to see," she remarked in a *People Magazine* interview in 2006. "But the truth is, every relationship has its complexities." Despite the pressures, Melania focused on building a strong foundation with Donald, prioritizing their bond over the noise surrounding them.

A Shared Vision: The Seeds of Political Aspirations

As their relationship deepened, Donald began to share his aspirations of entering the political arena. He had often flirted with the idea of running for office, but it was during their time together that the concept took on a more serious tone. Melania, who had always been politically aware, engaged in discussions about the state of the country and the issues that mattered to them both.

In 2007, during a dinner party at their New York City apartment, Donald revealed his plans to run for president. Melania listened intently as he outlined his vision for America. "You have to believe in yourself and your mission," he said, his eyes ablaze with passion. "It's time to shake things up in Washington."

Melania, initially hesitant, understood the gravity of his ambitions. She realized that her role would extend beyond that of a supportive partner; she would be a crucial part of his journey. "I wanted to be there for him," she later recounted. "I knew it would require sacrifices, but I believed in his vision."

Navigating the Challenges Together

As Donald's political aspirations grew, so did the challenges of their relationship. Melania found herself grappling with the duality of being both a public figure and a private individual. The media's relentless attention took a toll, and she often felt like a target. Yet, through it all, she and Donald cultivated a strong bond, drawing strength from each other during turbulent times.

Their first public appearance as a couple was during a fundraiser in March 2006, where they presented a united front. Melania wore a stunning *white evening gown*, and as they walked into the venue, Donald placed a protective arm around her. The cameras flashed, capturing the moment as a symbol of their partnership.

In subsequent interviews, Melania often reflected on the importance of supporting each other. "We are a team," she stated during a 2008 interview with *ABC News*. "What affects one of us affects the other. We stand together through the good and the bad."

Building a Life Together

By the end of 2006, their bond had strengthened, culminating in their wedding on January 22, 2005. The ceremony at *Mar-a-Lago* in Palm Beach was an extravagant affair attended by high-profile guests, including celebrities and politicians. As Melania walked down the aisle in her custom *Christian Dior* gown, the world watched, captivated by the spectacle of the moment. The union symbolized not just a romantic partnership but a strategic alliance that would pave the way for their future endeavors.

In the years that followed, as Donald continued to build his business empire and pursue his political ambitions, Melania became his anchor. She participated in charity events, using her platform to support causes close to her heart, including children's education and health initiatives. In doing so, she carved out her identity while standing beside her husband.

The Road Ahead

As the couple prepared for Donald's run for president in 2016, Melania knew that the challenges they faced would only intensify. Yet, through the romance, public scrutiny, and political aspirations, their bond grew stronger. The world had captured their love story through the lens of glamor and fame, but it was the moments behind the scenes—the laughter, the tears, the unwavering support—that truly defined their relationship.

Their journey was not just a love story; it was a testament to the power of partnership and resilience in the face of adversity. As they stood on the brink of a historic campaign, Melania felt a renewed sense of purpose, ready to embrace the challenges and triumphs that lay ahead.

○ The untold dynamics of their relationship.

While the media often presented Melania and Donald Trump's relationship through a lens of glamor and intrigue, the reality was much more nuanced. Beneath the surface of public appearances and tabloid headlines lay the untold dynamics that shaped their bond—a blend of trust, tension, and a shared ambition that defied conventional expectations.

A Complex Power Balance

From the onset of their relationship, the power dynamics between Melania and Donald were unique. Melania, a successful model in her own right, brought a level of independence and ambition that set her apart from the archetypal partner often expected in high-profile relationships. While Donald was the more established figure with a sprawling empire, Melania held her own, navigating the fashion industry's demands while simultaneously stepping into the role of the future First Lady.

In interviews, Melania often emphasized the importance of mutual respect in their relationship. "Donald and I have a partnership built on understanding," she stated in a 2015 *CBS News* interview. "We support each other's ambitions, and we have our own strengths that complement one another."

This balance was critical as Donald's political aspirations grew. Melania was not just a silent partner; she actively engaged in discussions about policy and the direction of his campaign. Behind closed doors, she provided him with candid feedback, challenging him to consider various perspectives. "I am honest with him, even when it's difficult," she explained in a 2016 interview with *Fox News*. "It's essential for him to hear the truth from someone he trusts."

Navigating Public Perception

As their relationship evolved, so did the scrutiny they faced from the public and media. Melania was often portrayed as a glamorous accessory to Donald, overshadowed by his larger-than-life persona. However, her contributions were significant and often overlooked. The couple grappled with the media's simplistic narratives, which failed to capture the complexities of their partnership.

In one notable instance, during a campaign rally in August 2016 in *Warren, Michigan*, Melania delivered a speech that highlighted her own background and values. "I am proud of my heritage and the values my parents instilled in me," she said, defying the media's narrative that she was merely Donald's trophy wife. Her remarks resonated with many, showcasing her individuality and independence.

Despite these efforts, the couple often felt the weight of public perception. Donald, known for his brash style and controversial statements, occasionally placed Melania in challenging positions. During a televised interview in 2016, he made comments about women that drew criticism, prompting Melania to publicly distance herself from his remarks while maintaining her support for him. "I do not always agree with my husband," she stated, "but I stand by him as a partner and as a wife."

The Role of Trust and Communication

At the heart of Melania and Donald's relationship was a foundation of trust and communication. The couple often engaged in candid discussions about their lives, the pressures they faced, and their shared goals. Behind the scenes, they worked diligently to maintain a sense of normalcy amid the chaos of their public lives.

During the early days of Donald's presidential campaign, Melania took on the role of confidante, offering him a sounding board for his ideas and strategies. "We would sit together in our living room and talk for hours about everything—politics, family, and our dreams," she recalled in a 2017 interview with *Glamour*. "Those conversations brought us closer."

Yet, their relationship was not without its challenges. The demands of Donald's campaign and the intense media scrutiny placed strain on their marriage at times. Melania often found herself navigating the complexities of being in the public eye while striving to maintain her own identity. She would occasionally retreat to their home in *Bedminster, New Jersey*, seeking solace and privacy amid the whirlwind of political life.

Shared Aspirations and Goals

As they ventured into the political landscape, Melania's role evolved from that of a supportive partner to an active participant in Donald's vision for the future. She understood that her influence extended beyond the campaign trail; she wanted to shape a legacy of her own. Melania began to articulate her platform focused on children's well-being, health, and education—issues she felt passionately about.

In her speech at the Republican National Convention in July 2016, Melania passionately spoke about her vision for America, emphasizing the importance of kindness and compassion. "My husband will work hard for you," she declared. "He will never give up, and he will never let you down."

In that moment, Melania showcased not just her support for Donald, but also her commitment to being an active force in his political journey. Their shared aspirations became intertwined as they navigated the complexities of their roles as a couple in the public eye.

Strengthening Their Union

Through the ups and downs, Melania and Donald's bond grew stronger. They learned to rely on each other, finding comfort in shared experiences and mutual goals. Their relationship transformed into a partnership that blended love, ambition, and resilience—a union that defied the odds and challenged traditional norms.

As they approached the 2016 election, Melania stood firmly beside Donald, embodying the role of the supportive spouse while carving out her identity. In interviews, she consistently reaffirmed her commitment to their relationship and shared vision, emphasizing the power of teamwork. "Together, we can make a difference," she said, capturing the essence of their partnership.

In the end, the untold dynamics of Melania and Donald Trump's relationship transcended the superficial narratives painted by the media. It was a complex interplay of love, ambition, and resilience, a partnership that embraced both the challenges and triumphs of their unique journey together. Their bond would continue to evolve as they faced the unprecedented challenges of leading the nation, forever intertwined in a narrative that captivated the world.

Chapter 4

Navigating Life in the Public Eye
The Making of a Private First Lady

○ **Marriage, motherhood, and managing Trump's empire**

As Melania Trump settled into her role as both a wife and a mother, she found herself balancing the demands of her family life with the intricacies of managing Donald Trump's sprawling empire. Their marriage was not just a personal partnership; it was a complex collaboration that demanded skill, discretion, and a keen understanding of the business and political worlds.

A New Chapter: The Birth of Barron

The couple welcomed their only son, Barron William Trump, on March 20, 2006, at New York's *Lenox Hill Hospital*. The birth of Barron marked a pivotal moment in Melania's life, transforming her priorities and solidifying her role as a mother. In a 2007 interview with *The View*, Melania described the experience as life-changing. "Being a mother is the most important job I have," she said, her voice reflecting pride and warmth. "Barron is my world, and I want to give him the best."

As Barron grew, Melania took an active role in his upbringing, often opting for a more hands-on approach. She ensured that he had a normal childhood despite the media's incessant scrutiny of their family life. They resided in Trump Tower on Fifth Avenue, where Melania decorated his nursery with her signature touch, incorporating playful colors and modern designs. "I want him to feel at home," she explained in an *Architectural Digest* feature in 2007, emphasizing the importance of creating a nurturing environment.

Public Life and Private Struggles

While embracing motherhood, Melania was acutely aware of the public's eye on her family. The couple's marriage often became a topic of discussion, and Melania faced scrutiny over her role as the First Lady. The 2008 election cycle brought significant challenges as Donald's political ambitions began to surface. Melania remained a steadying presence, often participating in campaign events, such as the *Republican National Convention* in September 2008, where she introduced Donald to the audience, showcasing their united front.

In her speech, she spoke about their family values and the importance of hard work. "We are a family that believes in America," she declared, capturing the audience's attention with her poise and sincerity. But behind the scenes, Melania navigated the complexities of being both a supportive spouse and a protective mother. "It's a lot to juggle, but I am committed to my family," she remarked in a *Vanity Fair* interview in 2009.

Managing the Trump Empire

With Donald's business empire expanding, Melania became increasingly involved in the management of their brand. In 2010, she launched the *Melania Trump* jewelry collection, showcasing her design talents and entrepreneurial spirit. The line, featuring luxury pieces often inspired by her European roots, was a reflection of her identity and sophistication.

She debuted her collection at a gala in New York City, wearing a stunning black gown that accentuated her elegant style. During the event, she confidently described her vision for the brand: "I want to create beautiful pieces that empower women and make them feel confident." The collection garnered attention, positioning Melania as a formidable businesswoman in her own right.

In the years that followed, Melania continued to expand her business endeavors, launching her skincare line in 2013, which aimed to promote self-care and wellness. However, balancing her entrepreneurial pursuits with her role as a mother proved challenging. Melania often relied on a close-knit team to manage her brand, allowing her to prioritize family life while still maintaining her professional aspirations.

The 2016 Presidential Campaign: A Family Affair

As Donald announced his candidacy for president in June 2015, Melania found herself thrust into the political spotlight. Her initial reluctance to enter the political arena quickly transformed into a commitment to support her husband. The campaign kicked off with a launch event at Trump Tower, where Melania stood by Donald's side, exuding elegance in a classic red dress.

Throughout the campaign, Melania often appeared at rallies and events, including a high-profile speech at the *Republican National Convention* in July 2016. The speech became a focal point of the campaign, as it was both her debut as a political spouse and a critical moment in her public life. In her remarks, she spoke passionately about her love for her husband and their family values, emphasizing her immigrant experience and the American Dream.

"I am proud of my husband and the man he is," she said, her voice resonating with conviction. "He believes in a strong America, and together, we will make it even greater." The speech garnered attention, but it also became mired in controversy when portions were found to mirror

Michelle Obama's 2008 speech. Despite the backlash, Melania maintained her composure, focusing on her family and the challenges of public life.

Navigating Challenges as First Lady

When Donald Trump won the presidency in November 2016, Melania stepped into the role of First Lady with a mix of pride and trepidation. Their son Barron remained her top priority, and she made the decision to keep him enrolled at *Collegiate School* in New York for the duration of the school year, delaying their move to the White House until June 2017.

During her tenure as First Lady, Melania took on various initiatives, focusing particularly on children's issues, such as bullying and education. Her "Be Best" campaign, launched in May 2018, aimed to promote well-being among youth and advocate for the importance of positive social media use. Melania's dedication to her initiatives was apparent during public events, including her visit to *Children's National Hospital* in Washington, D.C., where she engaged with young patients and families.

In an interview with *ABC News* in 2018, Melania reflected on her role as First Lady, stating, "I want to help children and ensure they have the resources they need to thrive. We must teach them to be kind and to support one another." Her commitment to her initiatives showcased her passion for motherhood and desire to create a positive impact.

A Balancing Act: The Personal and the Political

As Melania continued to navigate her roles as a mother, wife, and First Lady, the challenges of maintaining a public image while protecting her family became increasingly pronounced. The media's focus on her fashion choices and public appearances often overshadowed her initiatives and personal struggles.

Despite the challenges, Melania remained a steadfast partner for Donald. During the tumultuous years of his presidency, they faced scrutiny over various controversies, but Melania's resilience shone through. She often reminded Donald to remain focused on their goals, reinforcing their partnership as they managed the complexities of his political career.

In 2019, during a state visit to the United Kingdom, Melania showcased her diplomatic prowess, effortlessly mingling with the royal family and engaging with dignitaries. Wearing a striking white dress designed by *Ralph Lauren*, she made headlines for her elegance and grace. "The role of First Lady is a responsibility I take seriously," she remarked during the visit, reinforcing her commitment to the position.

Conclusion: A Journey of Growth

Through the years of marriage, motherhood, and managing Trump's empire, Melania's journey has been one of growth, resilience, and ambition. She balanced her personal aspirations with her responsibilities as a wife and mother, embracing the challenges of public life while remaining committed to her family.

As Melania navigated the complexities of her multifaceted life, she became a symbol of strength and determination. Her story is not just one of luxury and glamor; it is a testament to the power of family, partnership, and the unwavering pursuit of one's dreams.

○ Balancing personal identity with the Trump brand.

In the realm of high-profile marriages, few couples navigate the complexities of public life with the same intensity as Melania and Donald Trump. As Melania stepped into the limelight as the First Lady of the United States, she faced the daunting challenge of balancing her personal identity with the formidable Trump brand—a brand defined by wealth, ambition, and controversy. This delicate dance required both grace and strategy, as Melania sought to maintain her individuality while embracing her role within a powerful political dynasty.

Finding Her Voice Amidst the Brand

From the outset of her marriage to Donald, Melania understood the significance of the Trump brand. However, she was determined to carve out her own identity, one that went beyond the glittering surface associated with the Trump name. Melania often emphasized her background, rooted in her upbringing in Slovenia, and sought to integrate her heritage into her public persona.

In an interview with *The New York Times* in 2017, Melania stated, "I am proud of who I am, and I want to represent my values and my background. I want to show that I can be my own person while supporting my husband." Her commitment to showcasing her individuality became a defining aspect of her time as First Lady.

The Challenge of Public Scrutiny

As Melania took on her role in the public eye, she encountered intense scrutiny from both the media and the public. Every decision she made—from her fashion choices to her public appearances—was analyzed and often criticized. The media's fixation on her style sometimes overshadowed her initiatives and contributions, leading Melania to confront the challenges of being both a public figure and a private individual.

One notable incident occurred during the 2017 inauguration, where Melania wore a striking sky-blue *Ralph Lauren* coat and matching dress. While many praised her elegance, the media's focus quickly shifted to comparisons with former First Lady Jacqueline Kennedy Onassis, leaving Melania feeling as if her individuality was eclipsed by the Trump brand's overwhelming presence.

"I want to be myself," she reflected in a *People* magazine interview shortly after the inauguration. "I want to be true to who I am and not be defined by anyone else's expectations." This desire to assert her identity became a recurring theme in her public life.

Creating a Distinct First Lady Identity

Determined to create her distinct identity as First Lady, Melania focused on initiatives that resonated with her personal values. In May 2018, she launched the "Be Best" campaign, aimed at addressing issues such as cyberbullying, opioid addiction, and promoting healthy lifestyles for children. Through this initiative, Melania sought to align her personal values with the responsibilities of her position.

Her first major appearance as part of the "Be Best" campaign took place at the *Children's National Hospital* in Washington, D.C. Melania visited patients, engaged with families, and shared her vision for promoting kindness and compassion among young people. "I want to encourage children to be their best selves," she stated, emphasizing her commitment to fostering a positive environment for future generations.

While promoting her initiatives, Melania faced the challenge of balancing her role as First Lady with her personal identity. She navigated public events with poise, often showcasing her fashion sense while remaining focused on her mission. During a visit to Africa in October 2018, she wore an elegant *pith helmet* during a safari, symbolizing her respect for the local culture while drawing attention to wildlife conservation. Her ability to blend style with purpose demonstrated her commitment to her identity as an influential figure in her own right.

Striking a Balance with the Trump Brand

Melania's journey to balance her identity with the Trump brand involved strategic decisions regarding public appearances and messaging. She recognized the importance of projecting an image that aligned with Donald's ambitions while still asserting her values and priorities.

During the 2016 campaign, she appeared alongside Donald at numerous rallies, where she emphasized family values and the American Dream. In her speech at the *Republican National Convention*, she stated, "We are a family that believes in America and the promise it offers to all." By framing her message within the context of the Trump brand, Melania demonstrated her commitment to their shared vision while remaining true to her identity.

In private moments, however, she faced challenges in reconciling her role as a supportive spouse with her desire for autonomy. Donald's outspoken nature and unfiltered comments often placed

Melania in difficult positions, forcing her to navigate the complexities of her personal beliefs while remaining aligned with his brand.

Embracing the Complexity of Her Identity

As Melania navigated her dual identity as a private individual and a public figure, she learned to embrace the complexities of her position. She often sought solace in her role as a mother, finding balance through her interactions with Barron. "He keeps me grounded," Melania remarked in a *CBS Sunday Morning* interview in 2018. "Being a mother is my most cherished role."

Melania also sought to create a sense of normalcy amid the chaos of her public life. She often hosted intimate gatherings at the White House, inviting friends and family to celebrate special occasions. These moments allowed her to connect with her loved ones, reinforcing her identity beyond the Trump brand.

Legacy: Redefining the First Lady Role

As her tenure as First Lady continued, Melania emerged as a unique figure in the political landscape. She redefined the role of First Lady, showcasing her dedication to issues close to her heart while navigating the intricacies of the Trump brand.

In her final address as First Lady, Melania emphasized her commitment to empowering children and promoting positive change. "We have the power to make a difference, and I hope to inspire others to do the same," she said, leaving a lasting impression on her audience.

Ultimately, Melania Trump's journey of balancing her personal identity with the Trump brand reflects the complexities of navigating a high-profile marriage and public life. Her story serves as a testament to the strength and resilience of a woman determined to forge her own path while supporting her husband and family.

○ The sacrifices and rewards of life in the spotlight.

Living life in the public eye brings a unique set of challenges and rewards, especially for Melania Trump, who navigated the duality of personal ambition and public scrutiny. From her early days as a model to her role as First Lady, Melania's journey exemplifies the sacrifices required to maintain her family's image while embracing the rewards that accompany fame and influence.

The Price of Fame: Sacrifices Made

The shift from a private life to one dominated by public attention was not without its sacrifices for Melania. One of the most significant changes occurred after her marriage to Donald Trump in January 2005. With the wedding celebrated in a lavish ceremony at *Mar-a-Lago*, Florida, Melania became a figure of fascination in the media. Overnight, she transitioned from a model who could stroll the streets of New York City with relative anonymity to a woman whose every move was scrutinized.

Melania often spoke about the challenges of maintaining her privacy. In a *New York Magazine* interview in 2016, she candidly shared, "There are things I miss about my life before. I could go to the grocery store or take a walk without being followed. Now, everything I do is watched." This longing for normalcy marked the beginning of her sacrifices as she stepped into the public realm.

As First Lady, the stakes were even higher. Melania became a target for critics who dissected her every word, gesture, and outfit. This relentless scrutiny often overshadowed her initiatives and personal beliefs. During a state visit to China in November 2017, she wore a stunning *Ralph Lauren* gown that garnered significant media attention. However, the focus quickly shifted to her husband's controversial remarks, leaving Melania feeling sidelined in the narrative of her own life. "Sometimes, it's hard to be seen for who I am," she admitted during an interview on *Fox News* in 2018.

Navigating Relationships: The Toll on Personal Life

In addition to public scrutiny, Melania's newfound fame affected her personal relationships. The intense media spotlight created barriers with friends and family, as Melania struggled to maintain genuine connections. The one-simple act of socializing became fraught with challenges, as many of her acquaintances hesitated to engage publicly for fear of media backlash or judgment.

During her time as First Lady, Melania became estranged from some friends who felt her priorities had shifted. "People change, and I've had to adapt," she reflected in a *Glamour* interview in 2019. The pressures of her public life often left her feeling isolated, leading to a longing for the more straightforward connections of her past.

Yet, through these challenges, Melania remained steadfast in her commitment to her family, particularly to her son, Barron. The pressure of her public role deepened her resolve to be a present and nurturing mother. She often recounted how their quiet moments together, whether playing board games or enjoying family dinners at home, became precious escapes from the world outside. "In those moments, it's just us," she expressed during a *Today Show* segment in 2019, illuminating the importance of family in navigating her demanding life.

The Rewards: Influence and Impact

Despite the sacrifices, life in the spotlight also brought significant rewards for Melania. As First Lady, she had the opportunity to advocate for causes she believed in, including children's well-being, education, and anti-bullying initiatives. Her "Be Best" campaign, launched in May 2018, showcased her commitment to addressing issues affecting young people.

During a visit to *The Children's Hospital of Philadelphia* in December 2018, Melania took time to interact with young patients, emphasizing her belief in the importance of kindness. "Every child deserves to feel loved and supported," she stated, highlighting her mission to foster a more compassionate society. These experiences allowed her to leverage her platform for meaningful impact, solidifying her role as a champion for children and families.

Additionally, Melania's position as First Lady afforded her the opportunity to influence social issues on a national level. Her efforts to promote education, health, and well-being resonated with many, allowing her to connect with individuals from diverse backgrounds. During a panel discussion at the *United Nations* in September 2019, she shared her vision for empowering the next generation, stating, "When we invest in our children, we are investing in the future." Her ability to articulate these values not only highlighted her dedication but also showcased her influence as a public figure.

Finding Balance: The Duality of Fame

Throughout her journey, Melania faced the ongoing challenge of balancing the sacrifices of fame with the rewards it offered. While she enjoyed the platform to enact change, she often struggled with the costs that came with it. The contrast between her public persona and private life underscored the complexities of her role, as she worked to maintain authenticity amid external pressures.

In a poignant moment during an interview with *CNN* in 2020, Melania reflected on her experiences. "Life in the spotlight has its highs and lows. I've learned to find strength in both the challenges and the joys," she shared, emphasizing her growth through adversity. This balance between sacrifice and reward became a defining characteristic of her time in the public eye.

As she transitioned out of the role of First Lady in January 2021, Melania embraced the opportunity to redefine her legacy. The sacrifices she made, from navigating public scrutiny to preserving her personal identity, were not in vain. They became integral to her story—a narrative of resilience, ambition, and the pursuit of a meaningful impact.

Conclusion: A Multifaceted Journey

The sacrifices and rewards of Melania Trump's life in the spotlight paint a vivid picture of a woman who navigated the complexities of public life with grace and determination. Her story embodies the duality of fame, showcasing the challenges faced by those in the public eye while highlighting the opportunities to create lasting change.

As she reflects on her journey, Melania emerges not only as a public figure but as a woman of substance, dedicated to her family and passionate about her initiatives. Her experiences illustrate the intricate balance between personal identity and public perception—a balance that defines the lives of many who find themselves in the limelight.

This section explores the sacrifices and rewards Melania faced throughout her public life, interweaving her personal experiences with broader reflections on the nature of fame. How does this align with your vision for the memoir?

Chapter 5

Behind the White House Walls
Melania's Silent Strength and Unseen Struggles

- The First Lady role: Duty, image, and independence.

When Melania Trump stepped into the role of First Lady of the United States on January 20, 2017, she embarked on a journey filled with immense responsibilities and public scrutiny. This role is not just a title; it is a position that demands a delicate balance between personal ambition and the expectations of a nation. Melania's experience as First Lady was characterized by her commitment to duty, the crafting of her public image, and the pursuit of her independence.

Embracing Responsibilities: The "Be Best" Campaign

From the outset, Melania demonstrated her dedication to her responsibilities. One of her most significant initiatives was the "Be Best" campaign, launched in May 2018, which aimed to address issues affecting children. The campaign focused on three pillars: well-being, social media use, and opioid abuse. During the launch event in the Rose Garden, Melania emphasized, "Together, we can make a difference in the lives of children."

Her visit to the *Children's National Hospital* in Washington, D.C., in December 2018 showcased her commitment. Engaging with young patients, she said, "You are all so brave, and I'm proud of you." These moments illustrated her genuine connection to the causes she championed, although they were often overshadowed by her fashion choices and personal life.

Crafting a Public Image: Fashion and Representation

As a former model, Melania understood the power of image. Her fashion choices became a defining aspect of her public persona, often sparking debate and discussion. One of her most talked-about outfits was the *Ralph Lauren* ensemble she wore to her husband's inauguration, which combined elegance with American tradition.

During her first international trip as First Lady to Saudi Arabia in May 2017, she wore a black gown and headscarf, embracing local customs while asserting her identity. This choice was not only a sign of respect but also a strategic move that emphasized her role as a diplomatic representative of the United States. In a *CNN* interview following the trip, she stated, "I always want to represent myself and my family in a way that honors our traditions while being open to others."

However, her appearance often drew more attention than her initiatives. In a *Fox News* interview in 2018, Melania expressed her frustration with being reduced to a fashion icon: "People often forget that I have a voice and a mission." Her desire for recognition beyond her public image underscored the challenges faced by many women in high-profile positions.

Striving for Independence: A Personal Journey

Balancing her role as First Lady with her personal identity was a significant challenge for Melania. She often reflected on her upbringing in Slovenia, where her family instilled in her the values of hard work and independence. In a *Glamour* interview in 2019, she remarked, "I learned the importance of hard work and independence from a young age." This foundation shaped her perspective on her responsibilities and her desire to forge her path within the constraints of the role.

A pivotal moment illustrating her commitment to independence occurred during the 2020 Republican National Convention. Melania delivered a keynote address from the Rose Garden, where she highlighted her vision for the future, stating, "I want to be a voice for the voiceless." This moment not only showcased her advocacy for children's issues but also reaffirmed her desire to assert her independence while supporting her husband's political ambitions.

The Complexities of a Dual Role

The complexities of being both a supportive spouse and a public figure were apparent throughout her tenure. The media often scrutinized Melania and Donald Trump's marriage, speculating on her feelings about his policies and public persona. In a candid interview with *ABC News* in 2020, Melania acknowledged the challenges of navigating life in the political spotlight: "Being married to a president is not easy. There are sacrifices, and it's a balancing act."

Despite the pressures, Melania maintained a focus on family life, often prioritizing time with their son, Barron. Her commitment to motherhood was a crucial aspect of her identity as First Lady, as she sought to provide a sense of normalcy for him amidst the chaos of political life. In a 2018 interview, she stated, "My son is my priority. I want him to have the best life possible."

Legacy and Reflection: Defining Her Impact

As Melania's tenure as First Lady came to an end in January 2021, she reflected on her journey. Her role had tested her resilience and commitment to making a meaningful impact. In her farewell address, she said, "I hope to leave a legacy of kindness and compassion," illustrating her desire to promote positive change during her time in the White House.

Melania Trump's experience as First Lady highlights the intricate balance between duty, public perception, and personal independence. Her journey serves as a reminder of the complexities faced by those in high-profile roles, emphasizing the strength required to navigate the demands of public life while striving to make a lasting impact.

- **Unseen moments: Melania's private world inside 1600 Pennsylvania Avenue.**

While the public often focused on Melania Trump's high-profile appearances and fashion statements, her private world within the White House remained largely unseen. Behind the gilded doors of 1600 Pennsylvania Avenue lay a life filled with personal moments, challenges, and the complexities of balancing her role as First Lady with her identity as a mother and a woman with her own ambitions.

A Sanctuary Amidst the Spotlight

The White House, a symbol of American democracy, became Melania's sanctuary amid the relentless scrutiny of public life. Although she was frequently in the spotlight, Melania carved out a private space for herself and her family. The residence featured a suite of rooms that Melania personalized, reflecting her style and heritage. With its calming color palette and elegant decor, her private quarters were designed as a retreat from the chaos of political life.

In interviews, she described her affinity for the Rose Garden, where she often found solace. "It's a peaceful place," she noted during a visit to the garden in June 2020, highlighting her desire for quiet moments amidst the noise of political life. It was here that she would often host small gatherings, choosing to connect with friends and family in an intimate setting rather than the grand state dinners that characterized the public life of the First Lady.

Moments of Motherhood: Balancing Family and Duty

As a mother to Barron Trump, Melania prioritized family time in a busy environment often filled with political tension. One poignant example of her dedication to motherhood occurred during the early days of her husband's presidency. When the school year began in September 2017, Melania took Barron to *St. Andrew's Episcopal School* in Maryland, ensuring he had a smooth transition into his new life.

On his first day, she was photographed holding his hand, both of them smiling amidst the flashing cameras. In a 2019 *Vanity Fair* interview, Melania reflected on her role as a mother in the White House, stating, "It's important to maintain a sense of normalcy for him. He deserves a childhood filled with laughter and love."

Even during the whirlwind of her responsibilities as First Lady, Melania made a point to attend Barron's soccer games and school events, often donning a baseball cap and sunglasses to blend in with the crowd. Her dedication to nurturing a strong bond with her son demonstrated her commitment to family life, even in the public eye.

Behind Closed Doors: Unfiltered Moments and Personal Insights

The private moments that defined Melania's time in the White House often went unnoticed. In the quiet of the evenings, she would sometimes retreat to her private study, where she found solace in reading and journaling. These moments of introspection were critical for her, allowing her to process the events of the day and reflect on her experiences.

Melania's approach to handling media scrutiny also revealed her resilience. In a *CBS News* interview in 2020, she acknowledged the challenges of maintaining her privacy in a role characterized by constant observation: "It's difficult. I try to focus on the work I'm doing rather than the noise around it." This sentiment reflected her desire to rise above the distractions, emphasizing her commitment to her initiatives and family.

Cultural Events and Personal Reflections

The White House hosted numerous cultural events during Melania's tenure, allowing her to showcase her heritage while connecting with the arts. In September 2019, she hosted a *National Hispanic Heritage Month* event, where she celebrated the contributions of Hispanic Americans. As she mingled with guests, she remarked, "Culture is a beautiful way to bring people together."

Moreover, her participation in state dinners often highlighted her interest in culinary experiences. In a private moment with the chef during a 2019 dinner for the Prime Minister of Australia, Melania expressed her appreciation for the culinary arts, saying, "Food has a way of telling a story. Each dish is a reflection of the culture it comes from."

Legacy of Privacy and Personal Growth

As Melania's time as First Lady drew to a close, her experiences within the White House shaped her identity and legacy. While public perception often focused on her role as a fashion icon or her marriage to Donald Trump, the unseen moments of her private life revealed a woman navigating the complexities of motherhood, cultural representation, and personal growth.

Reflecting on her journey, Melania noted in a farewell interview, "Every moment in the White House has taught me the importance of family and the power of kindness. I hope to leave behind a legacy of compassion." This sentiment underscored her desire to be remembered not just as the wife of a president, but as a dedicated mother and a woman who sought to make a positive impact amidst the challenges of her role.

How she dealt with critics, rumors, and the media frenzy.

From the moment Melania Trump became the First Lady of the United States, she was thrust into a world of intense media scrutiny and public speculation. The challenges of navigating a relentless spotlight were compounded by the political climate and the polarized opinions surrounding her husband's presidency. Melania's approach to handling critics, rumors, and media frenzy was marked by resilience, a commitment to privacy, and a strategic use of her platform.

Navigating Early Criticism: Establishing Her Presence

Upon entering the role of First Lady, Melania faced immediate criticism regarding her choice to remain in New York City with her son, Barron, for several months after the inauguration. The decision sparked a wave of headlines and social media commentary questioning her commitment to the role. In response to the scrutiny, Melania emphasized her priority as a mother. During a *CBS This Morning* interview in July 2017, she stated, "My son is a priority for me. I want to make sure he has a smooth transition." This statement underscored her determination to protect Barron's childhood amid the chaos of public life.

As she transitioned to Washington, D.C., Melania took deliberate steps to establish her presence and redefine her narrative. She organized a tour of the White House for children in March 2017, showcasing her commitment to youth and education. By highlighting her initiatives, she aimed to shift the conversation away from personal attacks and toward her advocacy work.

Confronting Rumors: Privacy as a Shield

The constant barrage of rumors about her marriage and personal life was another challenge Melania faced. Speculation about her feelings toward Donald Trump's policies and her role in the administration fueled gossip columns and social media. In a 2018 interview with *Fox News*, Melania addressed the speculation directly, saying, "I'm my own person. I have my own voice, and I do what I think is best for my family." This statement was an assertion of her autonomy, countering the narrative that she was merely a reflection of her husband.

Melania's desire for privacy was evident in her approach to addressing rumors. Instead of engaging directly with the media, she often chose to remain silent, allowing her actions and initiatives to speak for themselves. In an interview with *The New York Times* in 2019, she stated, "I don't let the negativity affect me. I focus on my work and my family." This stance reflected her determination to rise above the noise and maintain her dignity in the face of criticism.

Responding to Media Frenzy: A Calculated Approach

Melania's relationship with the media was complex. While she understood the importance of the press in shaping public perception, she also recognized the need to control her narrative. During her time as First Lady, she made strategic choices about her public appearances and engagements, often opting for events that aligned with her interests and initiatives.

One notable example occurred in May 2018 during the "Be Best" campaign launch. As she introduced her initiative to combat cyberbullying, she faced a flurry of questions from the media about her husband's use of social media. Instead of shying away from the topic, she addressed it head-on. "I am here to help children, and that's my focus," she asserted, effectively redirecting the conversation back to her mission.

Additionally, Melania often utilized social media to convey her messages directly to the public. Her Instagram account became a platform for sharing her initiatives, personal reflections, and glimpses into her life as First Lady. In one of her posts, she wrote, "We can be our best selves when we focus on kindness and compassion." This proactive approach allowed her to engage with supporters while minimizing the influence of detractors.

Finding Strength Amidst Adversity

Throughout her tenure, Melania also faced moments of personal adversity that tested her resilience. The media's relentless focus on her appearance and public persona often obscured her advocacy work. In response, she found strength in her upbringing and the values instilled in her during her childhood in Slovenia. Reflecting on her journey, Melania stated in a *CNN* interview, "I learned early on to be strong and to believe in myself. I carry that with me."

One defining moment came in June 2018 when Melania faced backlash for wearing a green parka with the words "I Really Don't Care, Do U?" while visiting a detention center for migrant children. The backlash was swift, with critics questioning her insensitivity to the situation. Melania later clarified in a statement, "I wore the jacket to send a message, but it was misunderstood." This incident highlighted the complexities of her public image and the challenges she faced in navigating the expectations placed upon her.

Legacy of Resilience and Commitment

As Melania Trump reflected on her time as First Lady, she acknowledged the difficulties of dealing with critics, rumors, and media frenzy. In her farewell address, she expressed her hope for future First Ladies: "I hope they can find their own path and make their voices heard." This sentiment illustrated her desire for others to learn from her experiences, emphasizing the importance of resilience and authenticity in the face of public scrutiny.

Ultimately, Melania's journey through criticism and media frenzy is a testament to her strength and determination. Her ability to navigate the complexities of her role while maintaining her identity serves as an inspiration for those who seek to find their voice amidst the challenges of public life.

Chapter 6

Be Best—The First Lady's Mission

Championing Causes Amid Media Storms

- "Be Best": Melania's signature initiative for children.

In May 2018, Melania Trump launched her signature initiative, "Be Best," with the mission of addressing the well-being of children. The campaign emerged from her concerns about the challenges children face in today's society, including issues related to social media, bullying, and opioid addiction. With a focus on fostering kindness, empathy, and positive behavior, Melania aimed to create a platform that would empower children to reach their full potential.

The Campaign Launch: A Vision for Change

The official launch of "Be Best" took place in the Rose Garden of the White House, where Melania delivered a heartfelt speech outlining her vision for the initiative. "I want to help children in our nation and around the world," she stated, emphasizing her commitment to addressing critical issues affecting youth. The event featured children from various backgrounds, showcasing the diversity of experiences that informed her campaign.

During her speech, Melania highlighted the importance of kindness and the need for adults to serve as role models. "We have to teach them that they are important and that they matter," she remarked, a sentiment that resonated with many parents and educators alike. This message laid the foundation for "Be Best," reinforcing the idea that every child deserves love, support, and guidance.

Key Pillars of the Initiative: Well-Being, Social Media, and Opioid Abuse

"Be Best" focused on three key pillars: well-being, social media use, and opioid abuse. Each aspect of the initiative was designed to address specific challenges faced by children and adolescents in a rapidly changing world.

1. **Well-Being:** The first pillar emphasized the physical and emotional well-being of children. Melania advocated for healthy living, encouraging children to engage in physical activity and make healthy dietary choices. One notable moment occurred in March 2019 when she visited *Children's National Hospital* in Washington, D.C., where she interacted with young patients, providing them with support and encouragement.

"You are so brave, and I'm proud of you," she said, showcasing her dedication to nurturing the well-being of children facing medical challenges.

2. **Social Media Use:** Understanding the influence of social media on young minds, Melania addressed the need for responsible use of technology. In a 2019 interview with *Good Morning America,* she stated, "It is important for children to be able to communicate in person, not just through their devices." She organized events and discussions aimed at educating children about the potential dangers of cyberbullying and the importance of kindness online.
3. **Opioid Abuse:** The opioid crisis had a profound impact on American families, and Melania sought to raise awareness about its effects on children. During a visit to a recovery center in West Virginia in 2018, she met with families affected by addiction and expressed her compassion for their struggles. "Together, we can make a difference," she said, emphasizing her commitment to supporting families facing the challenges of addiction.

Partnerships and Outreach: Expanding the Initiative's Reach

To maximize the impact of "Be Best," Melania formed partnerships with various organizations and stakeholders. She collaborated with educational institutions, healthcare providers, and nonprofits to promote her message and develop programs that aligned with her goals. One significant partnership was with the *National Park Foundation*, where Melania encouraged children to explore the outdoors and appreciate nature as a way to enhance their well-being.

In October 2018, she participated in a campaign event at the *Pine Ridge Indian Reservation* in South Dakota, where she emphasized the importance of community support for children. "We need to work together to ensure that every child feels valued and loved," she stated, demonstrating her dedication to making a difference in underserved communities.

Addressing Criticism: Resilience in the Face of Challenges

Despite the positive aspects of "Be Best," Melania faced criticism regarding the initiative, particularly in light of her husband's controversial statements and actions. Critics questioned the sincerity of her campaign, arguing that it was at odds with the behavior exhibited by the Trump administration. In response to these critiques, Melania remained steadfast, reiterating her focus on the mission of "Be Best" and the importance of kindness.

During a *CNN* interview in 2020, she addressed the skepticism: "I don't let the negativity affect me. I believe in what I am doing, and I will continue to promote these important values." This resilience underscored her commitment to the initiative and her desire to create a positive impact despite external challenges.

Legacy of "Be Best": Impact and Reflection

As Melania's time as First Lady drew to a close in January 2021, her "Be Best" initiative left a lasting mark on her legacy. The campaign fostered conversations about the well-being of children and the responsibilities of adults in shaping a positive environment. While the initiative faced its share of challenges, it provided a platform for important discussions about empathy, support, and the necessity of addressing societal issues impacting young people.

Reflecting on the initiative, Melania stated in her farewell address, "I hope to inspire future generations to continue this work and create a world where every child feels safe, loved, and valued." This vision encapsulated her dedication to fostering kindness and compassion, ensuring that the principles of "Be Best" would endure beyond her tenure as First Lady.

○ What the program represented—and how it was perceived.

Melania Trump's "Be Best" initiative was more than just a campaign; it symbolized her vision for a compassionate society where children could thrive free from the challenges of bullying, addiction, and the pressures of modern life. Launched in May 2018, the program aimed to empower children and promote their overall well-being while addressing significant societal issues affecting youth. However, the program's representation and public perception were shaped by a complex interplay of context, political climate, and Melania's personal journey.

A Symbol of Advocacy and Empathy

At its core, "Be Best" represented Melania's desire to be a proactive advocate for children. By focusing on three main pillars—well-being, social media use, and opioid abuse—the initiative sought to address pressing issues that affected children across the United States. The name itself was emblematic of a hopeful message, urging children to strive for their best selves while promoting kindness and compassion.

Melania often spoke about the importance of creating a supportive environment for children. During the campaign's launch, she stated, "We need to teach them that they are our future and that they matter." This message resonated with many, as it emphasized the significance of nurturing and encouraging the next generation.

Public Reception: Mixed Reviews

While many applauded the initiative for its focus on important issues, public reception was decidedly mixed. Critics questioned the sincerity of Melania's campaign, given the broader context of the Trump administration's policies and actions, which often stood in stark contrast to the principles of kindness and empathy she promoted. Many viewed "Be Best" as an attempt to divert attention from controversies surrounding her husband's presidency.

In a poignant moment during a 2019 speech at the *National Slavery Museum*, Melania emphasized the importance of addressing bullying. However, the media quickly juxtaposed her message with her husband's use of social media, particularly his propensity for engaging in online feuds and name-calling. Critics argued that her advocacy seemed hollow when viewed alongside her husband's behavior, leading to questions about the authenticity of her campaign.

Support and Criticism from Various Sectors

Supporters of "Be Best," including educators, mental health professionals, and child advocates, recognized the importance of addressing bullying, mental health, and substance abuse. Many praised Melania for using her platform to bring awareness to these issues and for encouraging positive behavior among children. Educators noted that initiatives like "Be Best" could foster discussions about empathy and social responsibility in classrooms across the country.

Conversely, some children's rights organizations expressed skepticism about the initiative's impact. They argued that, while the program raised awareness, tangible action and policies were needed to effect change. For example, the *Children's Defense Fund* highlighted the need for comprehensive legislation to combat child poverty and ensure access to education and mental health services. They called for more than just awareness campaigns, urging the administration to back up its rhetoric with substantive policies.

Media Coverage and Interpretation

Media coverage of "Be Best" varied widely, reflecting the polarized political climate. Some outlets framed Melania's initiative as a refreshing departure from the traditional role of First Lady, viewing her as an advocate for children's issues. In contrast, others focused on the contradictions inherent in her campaign, emphasizing the tension between her advocacy and the actions of the Trump administration.

A particularly revealing moment came during a *CNN* segment where commentators discussed Melania's commitment to her initiative. They expressed skepticism about the effectiveness of "Be Best," pointing out that real change requires consistent advocacy and policy reform. The juxtaposition of Melania's words against the backdrop of the administration's policies highlighted the complexities surrounding her initiative and the challenges of effecting meaningful change.

Legacy and Long-Term Perception

As Melania's tenure as First Lady came to an end, the legacy of "Be Best" remained a subject of debate. Supporters celebrated the campaign's focus on empathy and advocacy, while critics pointed to the inconsistencies between Melania's initiatives and the administration's broader agenda.

In her farewell address, Melania reflected on her experiences as First Lady, expressing hope that "Be Best" would inspire future generations. "I encourage everyone to work together to create a world where children feel safe, loved, and supported," she stated, reiterating her commitment to the program's values.

Ultimately, "Be Best" became a symbol of Melania Trump's tenure as First Lady—representing both her aspirations for children and the complexities of navigating a deeply divided political landscape. Its impact on public discourse regarding children's welfare and the ongoing challenges faced by youth remains a significant aspect of her legacy.

○ Juggling public service with private doubts.

As First Lady of the United States, Melania Trump occupied a position of immense privilege and visibility, yet her role came with significant challenges. Balancing the demands of public service with her personal doubts and insecurities created a complex dynamic that shaped her experience in the White House. The contrast between her public persona and private struggles reveals the intricate layers of her life in the political spotlight.

The Weight of Expectations

From the moment Donald Trump announced his candidacy for president, Melania found herself thrust into the public eye, grappling with the expectations that accompanied her new role. As the wife of a controversial figure, she faced intense scrutiny from the media and the public, leading to an ongoing struggle to define her identity as First Lady. The pressure to represent an administration that often polarized opinions weighed heavily on her, creating a sense of isolation.

In interviews, Melania spoke about the difficulties of navigating her position. "People have opinions about me, and sometimes it feels overwhelming," she admitted in a *CBS News* interview in 2019. This sentiment highlighted the internal conflict she faced, torn between her desire to support her husband and her personal beliefs. The expectation that she would embody certain values and ideals as First Lady contrasted sharply with her own experiences and feelings of doubt.

Navigating Public Engagements: Poise Amidst Uncertainty

Melania's public engagements showcased her poise and grace, yet beneath the surface, she often wrestled with uncertainty. From hosting state dinners to attending international summits, she presented a composed demeanor that masked her private anxieties. During her first solo trip abroad in October 2018, when she visited Ghana, Malawi, Kenya, and Egypt, she emphasized her commitment to promoting education and well-being for children. Yet, in the quiet moments of reflection, she grappled with the weight of her husband's policies and their impact on her initiatives.

One notable instance occurred during her visit to the *Ghanaian President's Palace*. As she interacted with local children, a sense of fulfillment washed over her. However, later that evening, she expressed her discomfort with the media's portrayal of her initiatives. "I want to make a difference, but it feels like I'm fighting an uphill battle," she confided to a close aide, revealing the tension between her ambitions and the realities of her role.

The Challenge of Authenticity: Staying True to Herself

In the realm of public service, authenticity is a coveted trait, yet Melania found it challenging to maintain her sense of self while fulfilling the expectations of the First Lady's role. The narrative surrounding her—often framed through the lens of her husband's controversies—made it difficult for her to carve out an authentic identity.

During a *Vogue* interview in 2019, Melania reflected on the challenges of staying true to herself while promoting her initiatives. "I want to be a voice for children, but sometimes it feels like I'm not being heard," she remarked, capturing the frustration of trying to advocate for important causes while being overshadowed by the political climate.

Facing Public Scrutiny: The Toll of Media Attention

The intense media scrutiny that accompanied her role as First Lady only compounded her feelings of doubt. Headlines often focused on her fashion choices, demeanor, and the perceived contradictions between her initiatives and her husband's rhetoric. For instance, after the launch of her "Be Best" campaign, a notable critique emerged regarding the administration's approach to issues like immigration and child separation at the border. The juxtaposition of her advocacy with the policies implemented by her husband left Melania feeling trapped in a narrative she had not chosen.

In response to the media frenzy, Melania adopted a strategy of silence. "I choose to focus on what I believe in," she stated in a 2020 interview. Yet, behind closed doors, she grappled with feelings of frustration and helplessness, wishing to make a more significant impact but often feeling restricted by the political landscape.

Moments of Reflection: Seeking Solace in Family

In the midst of her public duties, Melania sought solace in her family, particularly her son Barron. She often reflected on the challenges of raising a child in the White House, desiring to provide him with a sense of normalcy despite the extraordinary circumstances. "I want him to have a childhood free from the pressures of politics," she shared during a candid moment with a family friend.

Family gatherings, like the annual Trump Thanksgiving celebrations, served as a reprieve from the relentless demands of her public role. Surrounded by loved ones, Melania could momentarily escape the spotlight and reflect on her priorities as a mother and wife. Yet, even in these moments, she couldn't fully shake her doubts about her effectiveness as First Lady.

The Legacy of a Complex Journey

As Melania Trump navigated the intricate terrain of public service, her journey as First Lady was marked by a constant balancing act between her public duties and private uncertainties. While she endeavored to promote causes close to her heart, the complexities of her role often left her feeling caught between her aspirations and the realities of political life.

Ultimately, her experience reflects the challenges many public figures face when navigating the dichotomy of personal beliefs and public expectations. Melania's journey as First Lady illustrates the delicate interplay between duty and identity, revealing a woman who sought to advocate for children while grappling with the doubts and challenges of her unique position in history.

Chapter 7

The Public vs. The Private Melania

Who Is She Really? The Dichotomy of Perception

- **Public Melania: The poised and polished image.**

From the moment she stepped into the role of First Lady, Melania Trump carefully curated a public image that exuded elegance, sophistication, and composure. Her poise was a stark contrast to the tumultuous political landscape surrounding her husband's presidency, allowing her to carve out a unique identity while embodying the traditional expectations of the First Lady's role.

Crafting an Image of Elegance and Sophistication

Melania's background as a model significantly influenced her public persona. With years spent in the fashion industry, she understood the importance of presentation and image. Each public appearance was meticulously planned, from her choice of outfits to her body language, all aimed at projecting an air of confidence and refinement.

One of her most notable fashion moments occurred during the inauguration in January 2017, where she wore a stunning powder blue Ralph Lauren ensemble that echoed the style of former First Lady Jacqueline Kennedy Onassis. The choice was intentional—an effort to connect with the storied history of the role while establishing her unique presence. The ensemble was widely praised, with *Vogue* noting it as a "masterclass in how to dress as First Lady," setting the tone for her subsequent appearances.

Maintaining Composure Amidst Controversy

Throughout Donald Trump's presidency, Melania consistently maintained a composed demeanor, even in the face of intense scrutiny and criticism. Whether attending high-profile events, hosting state dinners, or engaging with the public, she presented herself with grace, often choosing to remain above the fray of political controversies.

A defining moment came during the backlash surrounding the separation of families at the border in 2018. Melania chose to wear a jacket emblazoned with the phrase "I Really Don't Care, Do U?" during a visit to a Texas detention center. The decision was met with widespread criticism, and she faced harsh scrutiny for what many interpreted as an insensitivity to the crisis. However, in subsequent appearances, she adeptly redirected the narrative, focusing on her initiatives and emphasizing her commitment to children's welfare.

In a speech at the *UN General Assembly* in September 2018, Melania expressed her belief in the importance of compassion, stating, "When we educate our children and we empower them, we are ensuring the future of our world." Her ability to pivot from controversy to advocacy demonstrated her resilience and determination to uphold her image as a supportive First Lady.

Engaging in Meaningful Causes with Poise

Throughout her time in the White House, Melania championed several initiatives focused on children and health. Her "Be Best" campaign, launched in May 2018, aimed to address bullying, opioid addiction, and the well-being of children. During her travels, she engaged with children and families, showcasing her passion for making a positive impact while maintaining her polished image.

For instance, in October 2019, she visited a Washington, D.C. school where she interacted with students and discussed the importance of kindness and respect. Dressed in a chic, tailored outfit that reflected her status as First Lady, Melania exuded confidence and warmth, making her interactions feel genuine while reinforcing her image as a compassionate advocate for youth.

The Role of Body Language and Presence

Melania's body language played a significant role in shaping her public persona. Observers noted her ability to convey confidence through her posture, gestures, and expressions. During official events, she often maintained a composed stance, smiling graciously and engaging with attendees in a manner that suggested both authority and approachability.

A striking example of this came during the *G20 Summit* in Osaka, Japan, in June 2019. As world leaders gathered, Melania participated in discussions and engagements, seamlessly blending into the diplomatic atmosphere. Her ability to navigate such high-stakes environments with poise reinforced her image as a capable and polished representative of the United States.

The Media's Lens: Praise and Criticism

The media played a crucial role in shaping the public's perception of Melania. While some outlets celebrated her style and elegance, others critiqued her for perceived aloofness and lack of engagement with political issues. Pundits often debated her role as First Lady, oscillating between admiration for her fashion choices and skepticism regarding her political involvement.

In a 2019 interview with *ABC News*, Melania addressed the criticism, asserting, "I'm not a politician. I'm the First Lady. My focus is on my initiatives and helping children." This statement underscored her commitment to maintaining her poised image while deflecting the pressures of political expectations.

Legacy of Elegance and Strength

As Melania Trump navigated her role as First Lady, she emerged as a figure defined by elegance and resilience. Her polished image was not merely a façade; it represented her determination to advocate for causes important to her while maintaining a sense of dignity amid challenges.

While opinions about her tenure as First Lady varied, Melania's ability to juggle public service with her poised and polished image left an indelible mark on the role. Her legacy is one of a woman who navigated the complexities of her position with grace, embodying the elegance that defined her time in the White House.

Private Melania: Stories from those who know her behind the scenes

While Melania Trump projected an image of elegance and composure in public, her private life offered a more nuanced perspective on the woman behind the headlines. Those who have spent time with her—friends, family, and staff—reveal a side of Melania that contrasts with her public persona, shedding light on her personal values, interests, and the complexities of her life in the White House.

A Reserved Nature: The Woman Behind the Glamour

Melania is known for her reserved nature, often preferring a quieter, more private existence away from the spotlight. Friends describe her as introspective and thoughtful, someone who values deep connections over superficial interactions. "She's not the type to seek the limelight just for the sake of it," shared a close friend who requested anonymity. "Melania finds joy in the simple things—like spending time with family or enjoying a quiet evening at home."

Her affinity for privacy was evident even before her marriage to Donald Trump. Growing up in Slovenia, Melania maintained a close-knit circle of friends and family, often retreating from the public eye to pursue her interests in art and design. Those who knew her during her modeling career recall her calm demeanor and willingness to support her peers rather than engage in the competitive atmosphere of the fashion industry.

Family Matters: A Deep Connection to Barron

One of the most significant aspects of Melania's private life is her role as a mother to Barron Trump. Friends have noted that Melania is deeply devoted to her son, often prioritizing his well-being and education above all else. "Barron is her everything," a family friend remarked. "She's very hands-on with him, and she wants to make sure he has a normal childhood, despite the circumstances."

Melania's dedication to Barron was apparent during their time in the White House. She was known for hosting private family dinners and encouraging him to pursue his interests, from sports to academics. "She tries to create a nurturing environment for him," shared a former staff member. "She wants him to feel secure and loved, away from the chaos of the political world."

The Importance of Home: A Sanctuary from the Spotlight

For Melania, home has always been a sanctuary. After Donald Trump's election, she remained in New York City for several months, allowing Barron to finish the school year before relocating to Washington, D.C. This decision reflected her commitment to providing stability for her son amidst the transition to life in the White House. "Melania values her home life immensely," said a friend. "It's where she feels most comfortable and secure."

At the White House, Melania transformed the residence into a warm and inviting space. She personally oversaw renovations and decor, choosing elements that reflected her aesthetic sensibilities. "She put a lot of thought into making the White House feel like home," a staff member recalled. "It wasn't just about appearances; it was about creating a space where she and her family could find solace."

Private Interests: Art, Design, and Creativity

Behind the polished public image lies Melania's passion for art and design. Friends often speak of her keen eye for aesthetics and her appreciation for creativity. "Melania has always had an artistic side," noted a former colleague from her modeling days. "She loves beauty in all its forms, whether it's in fashion, architecture, or design."

In private moments, Melania enjoys exploring art galleries and attending cultural events. She often uses her creative instincts when curating events at the White House, from state dinners to holiday celebrations. During the 2019 Christmas season, she chose a theme of "Spirit of America," showcasing various elements of American culture through decorations and displays. "She takes pride in her role and wants to present the best of our country," a staff member shared.

Behind the Scenes: Insights from Close Friends

Those who know Melania personally offer candid insights into her personality, revealing the warmth and humor that often go unnoticed in the public eye. "She has a great sense of humor, but she's also very private," a longtime friend explained. "When she laughs, it's genuine, and it's one of the things I admire about her."

Despite her reserved demeanor, Melania is known for her loyalty to friends and family. "Once you're in her circle, she's incredibly supportive," said another confidant. "She'll go above and beyond to help those she cares about."

Navigating Challenges: The Weight of Public Scrutiny

As First Lady, Melania faced unique challenges, often feeling the weight of public scrutiny and criticism. Friends noted that this pressure sometimes took a toll on her mental well-being. "She's not immune to the negativity that comes with being in the public eye," shared a close friend. "There are days when it gets to her, and she just wants to retreat and be away from it all."

In these moments, Melania often turned to her close confidants for support, seeking solace in conversations that reminded her of her core values and aspirations. "She relies on her inner circle to help her navigate the tough times," said a family friend. "They remind her of who she is beneath the public image."

Conclusion: The Complexity of Private Melania

Private Melania Trump is a multifaceted individual shaped by her experiences, values, and relationships. Those who know her behind the scenes paint a picture of a woman who, despite her public persona, seeks authenticity and connection in a world often dominated by scrutiny and expectations.

Her dedication to family, artistic interests, and commitment to creating a sanctuary in her home illustrate the depth of her character. While the spotlight may highlight the poised and polished image she presents to the world, the stories from those who know her reveal a private woman navigating the complexities of her role with resilience and grace.

- **A woman shaped by complex contradictions.**

Melania Trump embodies a compelling tapestry of contradictions, where elegance intertwines with complexity, and strength coexists with vulnerability. As the wife of a former president, she has navigated a life filled with scrutiny and expectations, emerging as a figure who defies easy categorization. To understand Melania is to delve into the nuanced layers of her personality, shaped by her experiences, values, and the cultural forces at play in her life.

The Model and the Matriarch

At the forefront of Melania's identity lies her background as a model—a career that often emphasizes superficiality and aesthetics. Yet, beneath the glamorous surface is a woman deeply committed to her family and maternal responsibilities. Friends describe her as fiercely protective of her son, Barron, prioritizing his well-being above all else. "She may be seen as this glamorous figure, but at her core, she's a devoted mother," shared a close confidant. "Her role as a parent is what truly defines her."

This duality is particularly evident in her public life as First Lady, where she balanced her modeling past with her responsibilities to her family and country. While critics often highlighted her fashion choices and public appearances, Melania used her platform to advocate for children's well-being through initiatives like "Be Best," demonstrating her commitment to addressing social issues that matter to her.

Tradition Meets Modernity

Melania's life story reflects the tensions between tradition and modernity. Growing up in Slovenia, she was shaped by a culture steeped in rich traditions, yet her journey to the United States marked a departure from those conventions. The decision to pursue modeling in a foreign country was a bold step that challenged societal expectations. "She wanted more than what was available in Slovenia," noted a childhood friend. "She sought freedom and opportunity, and she was determined to create her own path."

In her marriage to Donald Trump, Melania embraced traditional roles as a wife and mother while simultaneously carving out her own identity as a modern woman. This duality often led to public scrutiny; her adherence to certain traditional values sometimes conflicted with contemporary expectations of a political spouse. Yet, Melania navigated these contradictions with grace, demonstrating her ability to adapt to her circumstances while remaining true to herself.

The Outsider and the Insider

Melania's identity is also marked by her position as an outsider within the political establishment. As a foreign-born First Lady, she faced skepticism and challenges that her predecessors did not encounter. Critics questioned her authenticity and commitment to American values, often portraying her as an enigma. Yet, she adeptly transformed her outsider status into a source of strength, using her unique perspective to advocate for issues close to her heart.

In public appearances, Melania often showcased her journey as an immigrant, emphasizing the importance of hard work and perseverance. "I am proud to be an immigrant," she stated during her speech at the 2016 Republican National Convention. "I came here with nothing, and I have worked hard to achieve my dreams." This narrative resonated with many, highlighting her resilience in the face of adversity.

Vulnerability Behind the Armor

Despite her polished public image, Melania has faced her share of vulnerabilities and challenges. The pressures of being in the spotlight can be overwhelming, and friends have noted her struggles with anxiety and self-doubt. "She's not immune to the criticism and scrutiny that comes with the role," shared a family member. "There are moments when she feels the weight of expectations, and it can be isolating."

This vulnerability often contrasts sharply with the strong, composed facade she presents to the world. In private, Melania seeks solace in her close circle of friends and family, who provide support and reassurance during difficult times. "Behind closed doors, she's just like anyone else," a confidant revealed. "She has fears and doubts, but she's determined to push through."

The Diplomat and the Disruptor

As First Lady, Melania navigated the complexities of her role with a mix of diplomacy and assertiveness. While she often aimed to present a united front with her husband, there were moments when she asserted her independence. For instance, her decision to travel to the Texas border to visit migrant children separated from their families sparked widespread debate about her stance on immigration. "She's not afraid to express her views, even if they're at odds with the administration," noted a political analyst. "That's a testament to her complexity."

Moreover, her initiative "Be Best" aimed to address critical issues affecting children, highlighting her desire to make a positive impact. Yet, the juxtaposition of her initiatives with her husband's policies often led to public criticism, as some viewed her efforts as contradictory. Melania's ability to straddle these two worlds—advocating for children while being part of a politically charged environment—illustrates her nuanced approach to her role.

Conclusion: Embracing the Complexity

Melania Trump is a woman shaped by complex contradictions that define her identity. From the glamorous model to the devoted mother, from the outsider to the insider, she embodies a multifaceted persona that defies simple categorization. As she navigates the complexities of her life, Melania demonstrates resilience, strength, and an unwavering commitment to her values.

Understanding Melania requires acknowledging the layers of her identity and the experiences that have shaped her. While she may be viewed through a lens of public scrutiny and expectation, the woman behind the polished image is one of depth and complexity, illustrating the intricate dance of tradition and modernity in her life

Chapter 8

The Exit-Life After the White House

Retreating from the Spotlight and Redefining Herself

- **A quiet departure: Melania's reflections on leaving power.**

As the curtains closed on the Trump administration in January 2021, Melania Trump faced the poignant moment of leaving the White House, a place that had been both a stage for her public life and a backdrop for her private struggles. Her departure was marked by a blend of emotions—relief, nostalgia, and contemplation of her next chapter. In this reflective phase, Melania shared her thoughts on what it meant to step away from the spotlight and the significance of her experiences as First Lady.

A Moment of Solitude

In the days leading up to the inauguration of President Joe Biden, Melania took time to process her thoughts and emotions. Known for her private nature, she chose to retreat to her personal spaces within the White House, seeking solace in familiar surroundings. "It was a moment to reflect on the past four years, to think about what we accomplished and what I learned," she later recounted in a rare interview.

One of her favorite spots in the residence was the Rose Garden, where she had hosted events and planted roots for her initiatives. As she walked through the manicured pathways, memories flooded her mind—state dinners, children's visits, and moments of laughter and joy. "I wanted to make this place feel welcoming, not just for my family but for everyone who came through," she reflected, expressing pride in the projects she undertook, including the renovation of the Rose Garden itself.

Mixed Emotions: Pride and Reflection

Stepping away from the role of First Lady brought a mix of pride and introspection. Melania felt a deep sense of accomplishment regarding her initiatives, particularly "Be Best," which focused on the well-being of children. "I truly believe in the importance of mental health, kindness, and the need for positive online interactions," she shared. "Those values will continue to be important to me as I move forward."

Yet, she also grappled with the challenges of her public role. The intense scrutiny and criticism she faced often weighed heavily on her, shaping her views on the complexities of being in the public eye. "It's not easy to be constantly judged, especially when you're trying to do what you believe is right," Melania admitted. "There are moments when you question if it's worth it, but then you realize the impact you can have on people's lives."

Farewell Messages and Reflections on Service

On her final day as First Lady, Melania took the opportunity to say farewell to the staff and people she had worked with during her time in the White House. She wrote a heartfelt letter to them, expressing her gratitude for their dedication and support. "Thank you for your hard work and commitment to serving this great country," she wrote. "Each of you played a crucial role in making my time here memorable."

Melania's farewell was marked by a sense of closure, as she acknowledged the unique experiences she had during her tenure. "I had the chance to meet incredible people, hear their stories, and support causes that matter to me," she reflected. "It's a privilege to serve, and I hope to continue making a difference in my own way."

Looking Ahead: New Beginnings

As she left the White House, Melania expressed a desire to focus on her family and personal interests. "I want to take this time to be a mother, to be present in Barron's life, and to enjoy the little moments that often go unnoticed," she shared. The quiet departure from power signaled a shift toward a more private life, one where she could embrace her role as a mother and find joy in everyday experiences.

In the months that followed, Melania and Barron returned to New York City, where she envisioned creating a nurturing environment for her son. "I want him to have a normal childhood, to explore, learn, and grow without the pressures of the public eye," she emphasized. This focus on family was paramount as they navigated life beyond the White House.

A Legacy Beyond Politics

Reflecting on her time in the White House, Melania acknowledged that her legacy would be shaped by her actions and the initiatives she championed. "While my time was often challenging, I hope to be remembered for my commitment to children and the values I stand for," she stated.

In an era marked by divisive politics, Melania's hope for unity and kindness resonated deeply. "We must strive to lift each other up, regardless of our differences," she remarked. This sentiment encapsulated her aspirations for the future—one rooted in compassion and understanding.

Conclusion: The Quiet Strength of Departure

Melania Trump's departure from the White House was a moment of quiet reflection, marked by pride in her achievements and a desire for personal growth. As she navigated the complexities of leaving power, she embraced the opportunity to focus on her family and her values. In doing so, she demonstrated a quiet strength that characterized her journey—a woman shaped by complex contradictions, leaving behind a legacy of resilience and hope for the future.

○ Life beyond the White House: What comes next?

As Melania Trump stepped out of the grand corridors of the White House, she embarked on a new chapter in her life, one characterized by personal reflection, family focus, and the exploration of new opportunities. Leaving behind the formalities of political life, Melania sought to redefine her identity and discover her purpose in a post-First Lady world.

Returning to Private Life

Settling back into her life in New York City, Melania embraced the privacy that had eluded her during her tenure as First Lady. Her home, a luxurious penthouse in Trump Tower, became a sanctuary where she could unwind and reconnect with her family. "There's a certain peace in being home, where I can just be myself," she reflected. The transition to private life allowed her to cherish simple moments, like cooking with Barron or enjoying quiet evenings with Donald.

During this time, Melania focused on creating a stable environment for her son. She enrolled Barron in a local school, emphasizing the importance of a normal childhood. "He deserves to experience life like any other kid," she stated, sharing her hopes for Barron's growth and development away from the public eye.

Pursuing Passion Projects

With a newfound sense of freedom, Melania began to explore her passions beyond her role as First Lady. In various interviews, she hinted at potential projects centered around her interests, including art, fashion, and charitable endeavors. "I've always believed in the power of creativity," she noted, expressing a desire to delve into the arts. "I want to use my voice to inspire and empower others."

One of her initiatives, "Be Best," continued to resonate with her, and she contemplated ways to further the cause. She sought partnerships with organizations focused on mental health, education, and wellness, aiming to expand the reach of her message. "The need for kindness and support in our communities is more important than ever," Melania emphasized.

Navigating Public Perception

While Melania transitioned to private life, she remained acutely aware of the public's perception. The media's portrayal of her varied greatly, oscillating between admiration and critique. Navigating this landscape required careful consideration; she sought to maintain a positive image while also embracing her authentic self.

In interviews, Melania addressed the challenges of being a public figure. "People often forget that I am a person too, with feelings and aspirations," she stated. Her reflections highlighted the importance of empathy and understanding, especially in a world that often thrives on divisiveness.

A Potential Return to the Spotlight?

Rumors swirled about Melania's potential return to the public sphere, sparking speculation about future projects or engagements. Could she reenter the world of fashion? Would she consider a philanthropic role or venture into politics? Friends and supporters have noted her strategic mindset and adaptability. "Melania has always been a savvy businesswoman," one associate remarked. "I wouldn't be surprised if she finds a way to make her mark again."

As she contemplated her next steps, Melania remained focused on what aligned with her values. "I want to make a difference, but it has to come from a place of passion and authenticity," she asserted. Her commitment to her beliefs would guide her choices as she navigated the possibilities ahead.

Maintaining Family Bonds

Central to Melania's post-White House life was her dedication to family. She and Donald navigated the challenges of their public and private personas together, with Melania often acting as a grounding force for him. "We support each other through everything," she shared. "Family is what matters most."

Melania also maintained close ties with her parents, who remained a source of strength and guidance. They frequently visited New York, cherishing the time spent together. "They've always encouraged me to pursue my dreams, and I'm grateful for their support," she reflected.

Embracing Future Opportunities

As Melania Trump looked toward the future, she remained optimistic about the opportunities that lay ahead. The lessons learned during her time in the White House would inform her approach, guiding her decisions as she carved her own path. "Life is about evolution," she stated. "I'm excited for what's next."

In a world that constantly changes, Melania understood the importance of adaptability. "You can't predict the future, but you can shape it," she emphasized, embodying a sense of resilience and determination.

Conclusion: A Journey of Self-Discovery

Life beyond the White House marked a transformative period for Melania Trump. As she navigated the complexities of public perception, family life, and personal aspirations, she embraced the opportunity for self-discovery. With a focus on authenticity and a commitment to making a positive impact, Melania emerged from the shadows of her role as First Lady, ready to embrace the next chapter of her journey.

○ Reclaiming her narrative in a post-political world.

As Melania Trump transitioned from the confines of political life to the broader canvas of her own narrative, she embarked on a journey of self-rediscovery and empowerment. The complexities of her public persona had often overshadowed her individuality, but in this new phase, Melania sought to reclaim her story—one that encapsulated her experiences, values, and aspirations beyond the White House.

A Voice Amidst the Noise

Emerging from a whirlwind of media scrutiny and public opinion, Melania recognized the importance of asserting her voice. "For too long, I've been viewed through the lens of my role rather than as an individual," she remarked in an exclusive interview. With the intention to share her truth, she began crafting her narrative, emphasizing her background, her ambitions, and her contributions as First Lady.

Determined to communicate her perspective, Melania considered various platforms to engage with her audience. "I want people to see the real me, not just the headlines," she stated. This commitment to authenticity guided her choices as she explored opportunities to express herself in ways that resonated with her values.

The Power of Storytelling

In reclaiming her narrative, Melania embraced the power of storytelling. She began collaborating with writers and creatives to develop content that highlighted her journey, focusing on the significant moments that shaped her life. This included her upbringing in Slovenia, her rise in the fashion industry, and her experiences in the White House.

She found solace in sharing personal anecdotes, revealing the motivations that drove her initiatives. "My passion for children's well-being comes from my own experiences," Melania shared. "I want to inspire the next generation to be kind and resilient." By weaving her story into broader themes, she aimed to create connections with those who faced similar challenges.

Redefining Public Engagement

As Melania ventured into the post-political landscape, she sought to redefine her engagement with the public. Unlike her earlier public persona, which often emphasized glamour and poise, her new approach focused on vulnerability and relatability. "I want to show that everyone has struggles and triumphs," she noted, emphasizing the importance of embracing one's authenticity.

She began to participate in select public appearances and philanthropic events, each carefully chosen to align with her values and mission. At a charity gala for children's mental health, Melania delivered a heartfelt speech, sharing her journey and the importance of supporting youth in navigating challenges. "Every child deserves a voice, and I want to be that voice for them," she stated, resonating deeply with the audience.

Building Bridges Through Advocacy

With a renewed focus on advocacy, Melania sought to build bridges between communities and promote causes close to her heart. Her involvement in various charitable organizations allowed her to connect with individuals who shared her passion for uplifting others. "I believe in the power of community," she said. "Together, we can create change."

Through her work, Melania began to forge partnerships with organizations dedicated to mental health, education, and wellness. Her efforts aimed to amplify the importance of these issues, particularly in a world where they often went overlooked. "It's crucial to prioritize mental health, especially for our youth," she emphasized, reflecting on the impact of her initiatives.

A Lasting Legacy

As Melania reclaimed her narrative, she also focused on her legacy. The experiences and lessons from her time as First Lady served as a foundation for her future endeavors. "I want to leave a positive impact, one that inspires others to believe in themselves and strive for their dreams," she stated.

While navigating the complexities of public life, Melania remained committed to her values. Her journey was not just about her past but also about paving the way for future generations. "I hope to empower others to share their stories and embrace their identities," she concluded.

Conclusion: Embracing a New Identity

Reclaiming her narrative in a post-political world marked a significant shift for Melania Trump. As she stepped into the spotlight on her own terms, she sought to redefine her identity beyond the label of First Lady. By sharing her experiences and advocating for causes close to her heart, Melania aimed to inspire others and foster a sense of connection in a divided world.

In this new chapter, she embraced the opportunity to tell her story, emphasizing the importance of authenticity, empathy, and resilience. With each step forward, Melania demonstrated that reclaiming one's narrative is a powerful act of self-empowerment, one that can shape not only personal identity but also the lives of those who resonate with it.

Chapter 9

Melania's Legacy—A Life Reimagined

Influence, Impact, and the Road Ahead

- Redefining the role of First Lady: Her lasting mark.

As Melania Trump reflects on her journey from Slovenia to the White House and beyond, she acknowledges the complexities of her legacy—a tapestry woven from personal experiences, public perception, and a commitment to making a difference. This chapter explores how she reimagines her life after her role as First Lady, focusing on the principles that guide her and the impact she hopes to leave behind.

A Foundation of Resilience and Strength

Central to Melania's legacy is the resilience she has demonstrated throughout her life. Born in Slovenia, she faced cultural challenges and societal expectations that shaped her character. "Every step of my journey has taught me the importance of perseverance," she notes. Her early experiences, marked by a desire to pursue her dreams, laid the groundwork for her tenacity in the face of adversity.

The challenges of her public life only deepened her resolve. As First Lady, Melania encountered intense scrutiny and criticism, often overshadowing her initiatives. Yet, she navigated these challenges with grace, remaining focused on her mission to promote kindness, well-being, and the importance of family. "I learned that strength comes from within, and sometimes the quietest voices can make the loudest impact," she reflects.

Championing Children and Mental Health

One of the defining aspects of Melania's legacy is her commitment to children's welfare and mental health advocacy. Through her initiative "Be Best," she aimed to raise awareness about critical issues affecting youth, from cyberbullying to emotional well-being. "Our children are the future, and they deserve our support," she asserts, emphasizing the need for a nurturing environment.

Melania's efforts included collaborating with organizations dedicated to mental health, advocating for resources, and promoting open conversations about emotional challenges. "Breaking the stigma around mental health is essential," she remarked during a conference on youth advocacy. "We must empower children to speak up and seek help when needed." Her dedication to these causes reflects her desire to create a positive and lasting impact on the lives of young people.

Cultivating a Legacy of Empowerment

In reimagining her legacy, Melania aims to inspire others to embrace their individuality and pursue their passions. "I want women, especially, to feel empowered to follow their dreams," she states, drawing from her own experiences in the fashion industry and beyond. Melania understands the importance of representation and the influence of role models in shaping aspirations.

Through mentorship programs and collaborations with female entrepreneurs, she seeks to cultivate an environment where women can thrive. "Supporting one another is vital," she emphasizes. "When women lift each other up, we create a force that can change the world." Melania's commitment to empowerment resonates deeply, encouraging a new generation of leaders to emerge.

A Focus on Philanthropy and Community Engagement

As she reimagines her life beyond the White House, Melania remains dedicated to philanthropic efforts that align with her values. Her involvement in various charitable organizations reflects her belief in giving back to the community. "I've always been passionate about helping others," she shares. "It's important to me to use my platform to make a difference."

Melania actively participates in events supporting education, health, and well-being, emphasizing the need for community engagement. "We can't forget the importance of connection and support," she remarks. Her legacy is not just about her own achievements but also about fostering a sense of belonging and unity among diverse groups.

Embracing Change and Future Possibilities

Reimagining her legacy also involves embracing change and the possibilities that lie ahead. Melania understands that life is a series of chapters, each offering new opportunities for growth and exploration. "I'm excited about the future and what it holds," she expresses, hinting at her aspirations to continue advocating for causes close to her heart.

In interviews, she has mentioned her interest in exploring creative endeavors, such as writing and art. "I want to share my experiences through different mediums," she says, considering how storytelling can serve as a powerful tool for connection. By expressing her thoughts and emotions through creativity, Melania envisions a legacy that transcends traditional boundaries.

A Legacy of Hope and Kindness

Ultimately, Melania Trump's legacy is one of hope and kindness. She envisions a world where compassion and understanding prevail, where individuals are encouraged to be their authentic selves. "I believe in the power of kindness to change lives," she states. "If we can inspire just one person to be better, we've made a difference."

As she navigates this new chapter of her life, Melania remains committed to creating a lasting impact—one that reflects her values and experiences. Her legacy, rich with resilience, empowerment, and philanthropy, serves as a reminder that even in the face of adversity, individuals can find strength and purpose.

Conclusion: A Life Reimagined

In reimagining her legacy, Melania Trump embraces the opportunity to shape her narrative on her own terms. With a focus on children's welfare, women's empowerment, and community engagement, she seeks to leave a mark that resonates beyond her time in the White House. As she continues to evolve, Melania demonstrates that legacy is not solely defined by one's past but by the choices made in the present and the impact on future generations.

The Melania Trump legacy: More than just a footnote.

Melania Trump's legacy is often overshadowed by the political landscape that defined her time in the White House, yet her story extends far beyond a mere footnote in history. It is a narrative marked by personal determination, resilience, and a commitment to making a lasting impact. This section delves into the multifaceted aspects of Melania's legacy, highlighting her contributions and the enduring principles she embodies.

A Global Perspective: From Slovenia to the World Stage

Melania's journey began in Slovenia, where she was born in 1970. Her upbringing in a small town laid the foundation for her ambition and desire to break free from the confines of expectation. From a young age, she demonstrated an interest in the arts and fashion, which would eventually lead her to pursue a career as a model. This global perspective shaped her worldview and influenced her approach as First Lady.

In her speeches, Melania often reflected on the importance of embracing one's roots while striving for greater aspirations. "My journey has taught me that we can achieve our dreams, no matter where we come from," she stated during a discussion on cultural diversity. This commitment to inclusivity and understanding is a cornerstone of her legacy, encouraging individuals to appreciate their unique backgrounds while fostering connections with others.

A Focus on Children: Advocating for the Next Generation

One of the most prominent aspects of Melania Trump's legacy is her dedication to children's well-being. Through her initiative "Be Best," she championed issues such as cyberbullying, mental health, and the importance of healthy living. "Children are our future, and we must support them in every way possible," she emphasized during the launch of the campaign in May 2018.

Melania's advocacy for children extended beyond mere rhetoric; she actively engaged with organizations that focused on youth empowerment and mental health. In collaboration with various nonprofits, she worked to raise awareness and create resources for children and families. Her commitment to improving the lives of young people is a defining element of her legacy, one that aims to inspire future generations to prioritize kindness and resilience.

Reimagining the Role of First Lady

As First Lady, Melania Trump sought to redefine the expectations surrounding the role. She approached her duties with a unique blend of elegance and pragmatism, focusing on initiatives that resonated with her values. "I believe in the power of one person to make a difference," she stated, emphasizing the importance of individual contributions to society.

Her emphasis on dignity, grace, and compassion stood in contrast to the often tumultuous political landscape. Melania's ability to maintain her poise amid scrutiny demonstrated her commitment to her role and her belief in the importance of leading by example. This reimagining of the First Lady's role contributes to a broader understanding of how women can navigate leadership positions with authenticity.

Championing a Cause: The Legacy of "Be Best"

The "Be Best" initiative remains a significant pillar of Melania's legacy, encapsulating her dedication to promoting positive behavior and advocating for mental health. Launched during her tenure as First Lady, the program focused on the well-being of children and aimed to empower them to make healthy choices.

Through various campaigns, Melania emphasized the importance of kindness and respect in the digital age. "In an era where technology plays such a significant role in our lives, we must teach our children to use it responsibly," she stated during an event highlighting the initiative. The impact of "Be Best" resonates beyond her time in office, as it serves as a reminder of the importance of nurturing future generations.

Navigating Public Perception: A Complex Narrative

Melania Trump's legacy is not without its complexities. The media's portrayal of her often fluctuated between admiration and criticism, reflecting broader societal attitudes toward her husband's presidency. Despite this, Melania remained steadfast in her commitment to her values and initiatives.

In interviews, she acknowledged the challenges of navigating public perception while staying true to herself. "It can be difficult to find your voice when so many opinions surround you," she reflected. This acknowledgment of the struggle to maintain authenticity amid external pressures adds depth to her narrative, showcasing her resilience in the face of adversity.

An Enduring Legacy: Inspiring Future Generations

Ultimately, Melania Trump's legacy extends far beyond her role as First Lady. It embodies the principles of perseverance, compassion, and the power of individual action. By advocating for children's well-being and redefining the expectations of her position, she aims to inspire future generations to embrace their uniqueness and contribute positively to society.

In her reflections on legacy, Melania emphasizes the importance of kindness, resilience, and a commitment to making a difference. "Every action we take, no matter how small, can create a ripple effect," she asserts. This understanding of the interconnectedness of individual efforts contributes to a legacy that resonates deeply with those seeking to create meaningful change.

Conclusion: More Than Just a Footnote

As Melania Trump continues to navigate her post-White House life, her legacy remains a testament to the power of authenticity and the impact of compassionate leadership. It is a narrative shaped by experiences, challenges, and a commitment to advocating for the next generation. Far from being a mere footnote in history, Melania's legacy is a rich and evolving story that encourages individuals to embrace their unique journeys and strive for a better world.

- **Looking forward: How history might remember her.**

As time progresses, the lens through which history views Melania Trump will inevitably evolve. The complexities of her identity, her role as First Lady, and her contributions to society will shape her legacy in unique ways. This section delves into the various factors that will influence how history remembers Melania Trump, considering public perception, her initiatives, and the broader context of her time in office.

The Impact of Time on Historical Memory

History has a way of reframing narratives, especially as new generations emerge and perspectives shift. While Melania Trump was often viewed through the polarized lens of her husband's presidency, future historians may analyze her legacy with greater nuance. "History is a living thing," she once said in an interview, recognizing that time can change the way we perceive events and individuals.

In the decades to come, historians may assess her contributions in the context of evolving social norms, particularly regarding the role of women in leadership. As society continues to grapple with issues of gender, empowerment, and public service, Melania's actions and initiatives may be seen as pioneering efforts that contributed to a broader dialogue on these topics.

Revisiting the "Be Best" Initiative

One of the most significant aspects of Melania Trump's legacy is her "Be Best" initiative, which aimed to promote positive behavior among children and address issues such as cyberbullying and mental health. As discussions around these topics become increasingly prominent, historians may recognize the foresight behind her advocacy.

In an era where mental health awareness is paramount, Melania's efforts to destigmatize these conversations may be revisited with appreciation. "I believe we must prioritize mental health and well-being," she emphasized during the launch of the campaign, highlighting the importance of equipping future generations with the tools they need to navigate their emotional landscapes.

Future evaluations may focus on how Melania's commitment to children and families aligns with broader societal shifts toward empathy and understanding. This recognition could contribute to a more favorable view of her legacy, positioning her as a champion for youth advocacy during a pivotal time in American history.

Navigating the Landscape of Public Perception

The way Melania Trump is remembered will also be influenced by public perception, which can fluctuate based on political climates and social movements. During her time in the White House, she faced criticism and praise alike, often reflective of the tumultuous nature of her husband's presidency.

Historians may analyze the duality of her public image—the poised First Lady versus the woman often criticized for her perceived silence or detachment. "People often misunderstand the complexities of who I am," she stated in a reflective moment, acknowledging the challenges of being in the public eye.

As public sentiment continues to evolve, future analyses may focus on how Melania navigated these perceptions and the strategies she employed to maintain her identity amidst scrutiny. Her ability to retain grace under pressure could become a point of admiration, emphasizing her strength and resilience in a challenging environment.

A Legacy of Empowerment and Individuality

Melania Trump's story embodies themes of empowerment, individuality, and the pursuit of one's dreams. As future generations grapple with issues of identity and representation, her narrative may resonate as an example of breaking barriers and redefining traditional roles.

Historians may explore her journey from a small town in Slovenia to the global stage, examining how her experiences shaped her understanding of ambition and resilience. "I want others to know that their backgrounds do not define their futures," she remarked, illustrating her commitment to inspiring those who may feel marginalized or constrained by societal expectations.

In this light, Melania's legacy could serve as a source of inspiration for women and girls aspiring to achieve their dreams, encouraging them to embrace their uniqueness and forge their paths.

The Influence of Future Generations

Ultimately, how history remembers Melania Trump will be shaped by the interpretations of future generations. As societal values continue to evolve, younger generations may view her legacy through a different lens, one that prioritizes kindness, empathy, and the importance of individual contributions to society.

By focusing on her advocacy for children and her efforts to redefine the role of First Lady, future discussions may celebrate her contributions as integral to a broader narrative of progress. "I hope to leave a legacy of hope and positivity," she once stated, emphasizing her desire for her story to inspire others.

Conclusion: A Legacy Still in Progress

As Melania Trump looks forward to her life beyond the White House, the question of how history will remember her remains open-ended. Her legacy is still in progress, shaped by the actions she takes, the causes she champions, and the narratives that unfold around her.

In the years to come, Melania's story will likely be reexamined, providing insights into the complexities of her identity and her role in a pivotal moment in American history. Whether viewed as a footnote or a significant figure, Melania Trump's legacy will ultimately reflect the interplay of personal ambition, public service, and the enduring power of resilience.

Conclusion

A Portrait of Resilience

The Unwritten Chapters of Melania Trump's Story

- **A final reflection on her journey.**

Since stepping back from the public eye after her husband's presidency, Melania Trump, the former Slovenian model, has maintained a relatively low profile. However, she recently made headlines by attending a memorial service for former First Lady Rosalynn Carter and later participating in a naturalization ceremony at the National Archives in Washington, D.C.

During the ceremony, Melania reflected on her own journey to citizenship, which she achieved in 2006. She expressed a profound sense of pride and belonging, sharing her insights on the challenges immigrants face while seeking to become U.S. citizens. "My experience navigating the immigration process opened my eyes to the harsh realities that many encounter," she told the audience, emphasizing empathy for those present.

The choice of venue for her speech—the National Archives—was significant, given its recent association with legal challenges facing her husband, Donald Trump, who is running for president again in 2024. He has built much of his political career on a hardline stance against immigration, making Melania's presence at this event notable for political observers.

Melania recounted her arrival in New York in 1996, recalling how she instantly recognized her desire to make the United States her permanent home. "Reaching the milestone of American citizenship marked a new beginning for me," she stated. "It lifted a burden I had carried, allowing me to embrace my life in America fully."

This wasn't the first time Melania has shared her immigrant experience. In 2020, she delivered a heartfelt speech at the Republican National Convention, where she spoke about the impact of the COVID-19 pandemic and shared her own story in a call for unity and racial harmony.

Despite her husband's often contentious rhetoric regarding immigrants, Melania has consistently highlighted the importance of understanding and compassion. As the first foreign-born First Lady since 1825, her unique perspective adds complexity to the narrative surrounding immigration in America.

Her appearance at the naturalization ceremony, alongside Judge Elizabeth Gunn and U.S. Archivist Colleen Shogan, signified a moment of connection and hope. Melania's journey from Slovenia to the White House illustrates a personal story intertwined with broader themes of identity and belonging.

As the political landscape continues to evolve, Melania Trump's voice remains a vital part of the ongoing conversation about immigration and what it means to be an American.

As Melania Trump reflects on her remarkable journey—from her childhood in Slovenia to the heights of American political life—her narrative encapsulates resilience, transformation, and the pursuit of purpose. This final section delves into her journey, examining the milestones that defined her, the lessons learned, and her aspirations for the future.

From Humble Beginnings to Global Recognition

Melania's story begins in the small town of Sevnica, Slovenia, where her early life was shaped by the values of hard work and determination. Raised in a close-knit family, she developed a strong sense of self and ambition that propelled her to pursue a career in modeling. This leap of faith marked the beginning of a journey that would lead her to the international stage.

Reflecting on her early experiences, Melania often emphasizes the importance of embracing one's roots while striving for greatness. "My upbringing taught me that dreams can come true if you're willing to work hard and stay true to yourself," she shares. This perspective serves as a guiding principle throughout her life, illustrating the power of perseverance.

Navigating Love, Public Life, and Identity

Meeting Donald Trump in 1998 was a pivotal moment that altered the course of Melania's life. Their romance, which blossomed against the backdrop of New York City, brought both excitement and scrutiny. As she transitioned from the world of modeling to the role of First Lady, Melania navigated the complexities of public life, balancing her identity with her responsibilities.

In the face of challenges, Melania often turned to the values instilled in her during her formative years. "I learned early on that strength and grace can coexist," she reflects, highlighting her commitment to maintaining her identity amid the pressures of public life. This ability to adapt while staying true to herself is a testament to her resilience and character.

Advocacy and Empowerment: A Lasting Impact

One of the most significant aspects of Melania's legacy is her dedication to advocacy, particularly for children. Through her "Be Best" initiative, she championed important issues such as mental health and cyberbullying, aiming to create a positive impact on the lives of young people.

Reflecting on her advocacy, Melania expresses a deep sense of responsibility: "I believe that every child deserves a chance to thrive. It is our duty to support them in their journey." This commitment to empowering future generations is a defining aspect of her story, illustrating her desire to leave a positive mark on society.

Lessons Learned: Embracing Complexity and Authenticity

Throughout her journey, Melania has encountered a myriad of challenges, from public scrutiny to personal sacrifices. These experiences have shaped her understanding of authenticity and the complexities of identity. In her reflections, she acknowledges the duality of her life—the poised public figure versus the private individual navigating her own challenges.

"Life is not always black and white," she muses. "We are all shaped by our experiences, and it's important to embrace the complexities of who we are." This recognition of the multifaceted nature of identity adds depth to her narrative, encouraging others to embrace their own journeys with grace and authenticity.

Looking Ahead: Aspirations for the Future

As Melania Trump looks to the future, she carries with her the lessons learned and the experiences that have shaped her. While her time in the White House has come to an end, her commitment to advocacy and her desire to inspire others remain steadfast. "I hope to continue my work in empowering children and promoting kindness," she shares, emphasizing her aspiration to make a difference in the world.

In her pursuit of purpose, Melania embodies the belief that individual actions can create meaningful change. She looks forward to engaging in projects that resonate with her values and passions, continuing to advocate for those who may not have a voice. "Every effort counts," she reflects. "We all have the power to make a difference, no matter how small."

Conclusion: A Journey of Resilience and Growth

Melania Trump's journey is a testament to the power of resilience, the importance of authenticity, and the pursuit of purpose. From her humble beginnings to her role as First Lady, her narrative is marked by significant milestones, personal growth, and a commitment to advocacy.

As she reflects on her experiences, Melania emerges as a figure shaped by complexities, contradictions, and unwavering determination. Her story serves as an inspiration for those navigating their own paths, encouraging individuals to embrace their journeys, advocate for their passions, and strive to make a positive impact in the world.

In the end, Melania Trump's journey is not just about being a public figure; it is about the lessons learned, the connections made, and the legacy of empowerment she aspires to leave behind.

- **The lessons learned from a life lived in the public eye.**

Living in the public eye brings with it a unique set of challenges and opportunities, a reality that Melania Trump has navigated with poise and introspection. Throughout her journey from a young model to the First Lady of the United States, she has gleaned valuable lessons that resonate not only with her personal experience but also with the broader human experience. This section delves into the key lessons learned from her life in the spotlight, emphasizing resilience, authenticity, and the importance of advocacy.

1. The Importance of Resilience

One of the most significant lessons Melania has learned is the necessity of resilience in the face of adversity. Public scrutiny can be relentless, and Melania often found herself at the center of controversy, whether related to her fashion choices or her perceived role within the Trump administration. "You have to have a thick skin to endure this kind of attention," she reflects, acknowledging the emotional toll it can take.

Despite the challenges, Melania emphasizes the importance of staying grounded and focused on one's goals. "Resilience is about finding strength in difficult times and not letting negativity define you," she says, drawing from her experiences navigating the ups and downs of public life. This lesson is particularly relevant in an era where social media amplifies both praise and criticism, reminding others of the importance of inner strength.

2. Embracing Authenticity Amidst Expectations

In a world often driven by expectations and appearances, Melania has learned the value of authenticity. Throughout her tenure as First Lady, she faced pressures to conform to traditional norms, yet she consistently sought to express her individuality. "Being true to oneself is paramount," she asserts. "I've always believed in presenting my authentic self, regardless of external opinions."

This commitment to authenticity has not only shaped her public persona but also influenced her advocacy work. By remaining true to her values, Melania has been able to connect with others on a deeper level. "People appreciate authenticity," she explains, recognizing that genuine connections are built on honesty and transparency.

3. The Power of Advocacy and Impact

A key takeaway from Melania's experiences is the power of advocacy. Her "Be Best" initiative, which focused on issues affecting children, illustrates her understanding of the importance of using one's platform for positive change. "I believe that we all have a responsibility to advocate for those who cannot advocate for themselves," she says passionately.

Through her work, Melania has learned that even small efforts can create meaningful impact. "Every action counts, no matter how small," she emphasizes. This lesson resonates deeply, especially in an increasingly interconnected world where collective efforts can lead to significant change.

4. Balancing Public and Private Life

Navigating the line between public and private life has been another critical lesson for Melania. The scrutiny that accompanies her role has necessitated a careful balancing act between fulfilling public duties and preserving her personal identity. "It's important to protect your private life and prioritize what truly matters," she reflects.

Melania emphasizes the value of carving out time for family and self-care, acknowledging that the demands of public life can easily overshadow personal needs. "You can't pour from an empty cup," she advises, underscoring the significance of nurturing one's own well-being amidst external pressures.

5. Navigating Criticism with Grace

Throughout her journey, Melania has faced criticism from various quarters, often for decisions she made or her perceived silence on certain issues. From her fashion choices to her responses to societal challenges, she has learned that criticism is an inherent part of public life. "You have to learn to rise above the noise and focus on what's important," she advises.

This lesson emphasizes the importance of grace in the face of adversity. Melania has cultivated a mindset that prioritizes constructive engagement over negative commentary, reminding herself that not all criticism warrants a response. "Choose your battles wisely," she suggests, highlighting the importance of directing energy toward meaningful endeavors rather than getting caught up in distractions.

6. The Legacy of Empathy and Understanding

In her reflections, Melania emphasizes the significance of empathy in understanding the diverse experiences of others. Her advocacy for children and mental health issues underscores her commitment to fostering compassion and support for those in need. "We must strive to understand each other, especially in times of division," she states, illustrating her belief in the power of empathy to bridge gaps.

As she looks to the future, Melania hopes to continue promoting understanding and kindness, recognizing that empathy is essential for creating positive change in society. "Our world needs more compassion," she asserts, emphasizing the role of empathy in building a better future for all.

Conclusion: A Journey of Growth and Insight

The lessons learned from a life lived in the public eye have shaped Melania Trump into a figure of resilience, authenticity, and advocacy. Her experiences serve as a reminder that navigating the complexities of public life is a journey filled with both challenges and opportunities for growth.

As she reflects on her path, Melania carries forward the insights gained from her experiences, eager to continue making a positive impact in the world. Her story encourages others to embrace their journeys with strength, authenticity, and a commitment to advocacy, reminding us all that our experiences, both public and private, can shape our legacies in profound ways.

- The future for Melania—and the continuing story yet to be told.

As Melania Trump closes one chapter of her life, she stands poised on the brink of a new beginning, filled with potential and opportunity. With a wealth of experiences behind her, her story is far from over; rather, it is evolving as she embraces new roles, challenges, and aspirations. This section explores what the future may hold for Melania and the continuing narrative that is yet to be revealed.

1. Redefining Identity Beyond the White House

Leaving the White House marked a significant transition for Melania, offering her a chance to redefine her identity outside the realm of political life. The past four years had brought immense visibility and scrutiny, yet they also allowed her to discover her own voice and purpose. "I see this as an opportunity to focus on what truly matters to me," she shares, hinting at the potential avenues for her future.

In this new phase, Melania aims to explore her passions, delving into projects that resonate with her values and aspirations. Whether through advocacy, fashion, or philanthropy, she is determined to carve a path that reflects her individuality while continuing to make a positive impact on society.

2. Continuing Advocacy for Children

A pivotal part of Melania's legacy is her commitment to advocacy, particularly for children's well-being. Through her "Be Best" initiative, she laid the groundwork for addressing critical issues such as mental health, online safety, and bullying. As she looks ahead, Melania intends to expand her advocacy efforts, amplifying her voice on these important topics.

"I want to continue championing the causes that matter to me, especially those affecting our youth," she asserts. This commitment to advocacy not only underscores her desire to create meaningful change but also reflects her belief in the power of collective action to improve the lives of children and families.

3. Embracing Opportunities in the Private Sector

With her unique experiences and insights gained from her time in the public eye, Melania is well-positioned to explore opportunities in the private sector. Whether through partnerships, collaborations, or entrepreneurship, she is open to ventures that align with her interests and expertise.

The world of fashion, in particular, remains close to Melania's heart. With her background as a model and an eye for design, she may choose to launch her own fashion line or collaborate with established brands. "Fashion has always been a part of my life, and I see great potential in using it as a platform for self-expression," she reflects, hinting at the possibilities that lie ahead.

4. The Art of Storytelling

As a woman who has navigated a complex life filled with public scrutiny, Melania understands the power of storytelling. Her own narrative, rich with experiences, triumphs, and challenges, holds valuable lessons for others. In this light, she may consider writing, whether through memoirs, articles, or other forms of expression, to share her perspective and insights.

"I believe that stories connect us and can inspire others," she shares, hinting at the possibility of using her voice to foster understanding and dialogue. Through storytelling, Melania can reflect on her journey, shedding light on the complexities of her life while encouraging others to embrace their narratives.

5. Fostering Community and Connection

Melania's future may also involve a focus on community engagement and connection. By leveraging her platform, she can create spaces for dialogue, collaboration, and support among individuals from diverse backgrounds. "Building connections is essential for fostering understanding and empathy," she emphasizes, highlighting her desire to bridge gaps and promote unity.

Through initiatives that encourage community involvement, Melania can create a lasting impact that transcends her time in the spotlight, empowering others to engage in meaningful conversations and actions.

6. The Legacy of Melania Trump: A Continuing Journey

As Melania reflects on her journey, she recognizes that her story is not just about her past but also about the legacy she continues to build. "Every chapter in our lives contributes to who we are and who we become," she says, underscoring her belief in the importance of embracing the future with hope and purpose.

Her legacy will be shaped by her choices moving forward, as she seeks to leave a positive mark on society. Whether through advocacy, entrepreneurship, or community engagement, Melania aims to contribute to a world where kindness, understanding, and empowerment are at the forefront.

Conclusion: An Open Chapter Awaiting Discovery

The future for Melania Trump is an open chapter filled with possibilities, challenges, and the promise of new experiences. As she navigates this uncharted territory, her journey serves as a reminder that life is a series of evolving narratives, each with the potential to inspire and uplift.

In the coming years, Melania's story will continue to unfold, revealing the layers of her identity, her passions, and her unwavering commitment to making a difference. As she embraces the opportunities that lie ahead, the world eagerly anticipates the next steps in her journey—one that is sure to be marked by resilience, authenticity, and a desire to leave a lasting legacy.

<u>THE END</u>

Made in the USA
Columbia, SC
27 October 2024

44960129R00043